continued . . .

"As a college athlete turned entrepreneur, what I learned leading teams on the field in competition has been more valuable to me than anything I learned in business school. Packard's *New Rules of the Game* gives practical insight that we all can learn from."
—Gina Bianchini, founder and CEO of Mightybell; cofounder of LeanIn.org

"When I read Susan Packard's *New Rules of the Game*, I found many relatable truths. In our family we did not list them as 'rules,' but we learned by my mother's example difficult balancing acts, like being gracious while staying cool, and showing grit while valuing being likeable to others, and if you fail, learn from it and try again. I live many of Packard's 'rules of gamesmanship' through my mother's wise examples." —Rachael Ray

"The similarities between business and athletics are profound. Finding comfort competing, the importance of practicing many roles on a team, and the key role that resilience plays—these define a winning spirit. Susan's book will be extremely useful to all women navigating career choices."
—Margo Georgiadis, President, Americas for Google

"I definitely think Susan is onto something here—the business world is all about competition, and while there must be winners and losers in the great game of life, being a competitor does not mean you have to sacrifice your femininity or become less 'authentic' to win. You just need to understand the rules of the game, and choose a strategic but comfortable method of playing within (or slightly bending) the rules. Susan's practical tips ensure that we're mindful of the game and how it's played to formulate a personal winning strategy."
—Marisa Drew, cohead of European banking for Credit Suisse

"Much like *Woman to Woman*, the first talk show for women that I produced, Susan's book is real life—real stories about how Susan and others she interviewed had the passion, competitive spirit, and grit to advance. It's a captivating read."

—Pat Mitchell, executive vice chair of the Paley Center for Media

"Susan Packard has written a fantastic book and roadmap for women to win in the workplace, by building their support networks and embracing competition. Susan and I competed, became friends, and built a trusting relationship during our time at CNBC. Her strength and skill shine through in *New Rules of the Game*. This book provides actionable steps for success in business."

—David Zaslav, president and CEO of Discovery Communications

"I first heard Susan Packard share her career advice at a small executive women's event I organized. She was inspirational, pragmatic, and frank. In her book, Susan helps women understand how gamesmanship can become another language to help one increase career success, without compromising one's authenticity."

—Dr. Ines Wilchert, copresident of Professional Women's Network Global, London City Network, and author of *Where Have All the Senior Women Gone?*

NEW RULES
of the
GAME

10 Strategies for Women in the Workplace

SUSAN PACKARD

PRENTICE HALL PRESS

PRENTICE HALL PRESS
Published by the Penguin Group
Penguin Group (USA) LLC
375 Hudson Street, New York, New York 10014

USA • Canada • UK • Ireland • Australia • New Zealand • India • South Africa • China

penguin.com

A Penguin Random House Company

PRENTICE HALL PRESS is a trademark of Penguin Group (USA) LLC.

Library of Congress Cataloging-in-Publication Data

Packard, Susan.
New rules of the game : 10 strategies for women in the workplace / Susan Packard.— First edition.
pages   cm
Includes bibliographical references and index.
ISBN 978-0-7352-0537-6 (hardback)
1. Women executives.   2. Career development.   3. Women—Vocational guidance.
4. Success in business.   I. Title.
HD6054.3.P33 2015
650.1082—dc23   2014040063

First edition: February 2015

PRINTED IN THE UNITED STATES OF AMERICA

10 9 8 7 6 5 4 3 2 1

Text design by Laura K. Corless

To my sister, Linda, who lived to dance, laugh, and love.

To Andrew, whose competitive fire couldn't help
but earn him a slot in college athletics.
He inspired me to write this book.

And to Bill, the best coach a girl could ask for.

Contents

Foreword

Some LEADERS are born WOMEN.

GERALDINE FERRARO
1984 vice presidential candidate

Geraldine Ferraro's fighting-spirit quote became a rallying cry for many of us in business in the 1980s. Things were truly changing, or so we thought.

More and more women were penetrating the hierarchy in all of the business sectors. It seemed just a matter of time until we reached a critical mass in the leadership ranks . . . and when that happened, the gender differences in style and temperament that so strapped us (or that we were effectively hiding) would no longer be an issue. The cultures would change and the businesses would thrive.

Clearly that didn't happen. What did change, however, is that today women can go as far in business as *they* choose to. There are just two requirements:

Find a business culture that supports your talents and skills.
Learn the language of gamesmanship that it takes to succeed in that culture.

The latter is what this book is about.

It is written by a woman who knows of what she speaks.

Susan Packard was a member of the founding team, and the only woman, at Scripps Networks Interactive (NYSE: SNI) when the company launched the HGTV cable network in 1994. In 1997 Scripps acquired the Food Network. The founding team went on to build both entities into multibillion-dollar businesses.

I first met Susan when I joined the Food Network in 1998. I had known her by reputation for years. She was the industry's ranking woman in the rough-and-tumble, totally male-dominated world of affiliate sales. She played the game with great skill, great guts, and unbelievable perseverance. She became HGTV's chief operating officer, with responsibility for the sales groups, marketing, and international and new business development.

I assumed in order to accomplish these things Susan would be one of those edgy and desensitized women who seemed to prevail at the time.

I couldn't have been more wrong.

I was taken totally by surprise by her openness, her support, and her willingness to share information, which is, of course, where the power always lies.

I was also very taken with her passion for building a culture that supported and prepared women for power positions, while recognizing women generally are not motivated solely by competition and power. Women bring other attributes into the workplace, such as collaboration and management prowess. Susan intended to fully use those strengths as building blocks for the business.

With that in mind, Susan guided the business into a set of declared core values that are still in place today. These values include compassion and support, openness, shared responsibility, and work–

life balance. And, of course, all employees benefit, as does the company. Scripps is ranked among the best cable networks to work at in every survey.

Susan also held regularly scheduled women's gatherings that were informal and off the record. Women from all over the company would gather with her and the other managers and talk about their challenges, their shortcomings, and the ins and outs of the gender gap we were all experiencing. It was a wonderful way for us all to become mentors to one another and share experience and wisdom without any regard to titles and rank.

Perhaps her biggest contribution and legacy, however, will be the lessons she shares in this book. It's the recognition that business is like any institution, and as such we, as women, need to understand the rules, behaviors, and norms if we want to advance there. Then, when we clear the field from middle management into positions of authority, we can—and should—make business a more matriarchal place. Her book gives us practical lessons to become leaders and, as such, is a huge step forward. In this book we can find that whatever we choose to achieve is truly in our grasp.

—Judy Girard, president of the
Food Network (2000–2005) and
HGTV Network (2006–2008)

Introduction

In 1956, twelve-year-old Joan Cronan decided to compete. She was a great little baseball player in south Louisiana, where she grew up. She knew she was good because she'd often beat the boys who'd come to play in her backyard. She asked local coaches if she could try out for Little League instead of girls' softball. She was told no. But it'd be OK if she were scorekeeper or cheerleader.

She went on to play the sports that were acceptable for women—volleyball, tennis, and golf. She pursued a career in the business of athletics and, at the peak of her career in 2011, rose to become the head of all sports programs—men's and women's—as the University of Tennessee's athletic director. She is the only woman to ever hold that position in the Southeastern Conference (SEC)—the most powerful football conference in the nation. And football is where the money lies in college athletics.

After three decades serving UT sports and a season at its highest position, Joan retired in the summer of 2014.

From backyard baseball to big-time college athletics, Joan had no trouble competing against boys. In fact she loved it. She thrived on it. And the question I raise is, Why? Why are some women comfortable with competition and showing the world what they've got while others are not? This book is about employing lessons from the love of games and competition to advance in your career. I want to help women learn how to unleash their competitive spirits and win. I call those who do this—women like Joan—*gamers*, and what they practice, the art of gamesmanship.

In our popular culture today, the word *gamer* has become synonymous with playing video games, but in this book I'm using it in a much broader context—a competition context. Simply put, a gamer loves to compete, and more often than not, she wins.

WHAT IS GAMESMANSHIP?

Gamesmanship is my word for a broad, strategic, and overarching approach to success in the workplace. It is something we practice every day in sports—and in business. It occurs whenever there's a competition with at least one other person. When we played board games or video games or even hopscotch as kids, we were engaged in gamesmanship. Organized sports are perhaps the most common form of gamesmanship, but it occurs anytime we compete. And it occurs endlessly in business.

The concept of gamesmanship is hardly new to the business world. It's not a coincidence that game-playing metaphors have invaded the business workplace. Our colleagues are our "teammates"; our goals revolve around "winning" that new deal or promotion; the "competitors" are others in our industry; we need to "practice" our presentations or skill-building techniques. We "roll the dice," we "raise the stakes," we "punt" on a deal we don't like, and we're urged to always "cross the finish line." In a cover article of the April 8, 2013, issue of *Fortune* titled "Rivalry," the writers highlight the greatest business competitions of all time, including Coke vs. Pepsi, Ford vs. GM, and Nike vs. Reebok. Business leaders think in terms of competitions and winning. I know I did, and it got me to the corner office of a large, successful company that today has a market cap of over $12 billion.

Gamesmanship asks that we view the workplace the way most men do, as one giant playing field with women and men running around on it. Sometimes we're in competition with them, and other times we collaborate. Business functions very much like a team sport. If you're a pro pitcher, you compete with the other pitchers on your team for a slot in the starting rotation. But when the game's on the line it's all about the team, and any internal competitions fall away. Everyone on the field goes for the team win. Good gamers are on board to rally and fiercely compete for their company, just as athletes are for their team.

As an individual on the team, there are big and small wins, and they change every day. They can be anything from the big things (a promotion or raise or acquiring new resources to do your job) to day-to-day matters (securing a meeting with someone of influence or even booking your favorite conference room). You know you're a gamer—one who uses gamesmanship mindfully, with purpose, to move up in the workplace—when something happens at work that you orchestrated, and your reaction is an under-the-breath yes! and a subtle fist pump. The win is always about moving our careers and our companies to the next level of success. We cultivate strength, creativity, and focus through the practice of gamesmanship. We learn to become better problem solvers.

Games are already showing themselves to be far more than fun; they indicate who we are and what we can do. In her 2010 TED talk, Dr. Jane McGonigal from the Institute for the Future described four traits of video gamers:

- **Urgent optimism:** Gamers act immediately to tackle a challenge.
- **Social connectedness:** Gamers connect with others and build up social relationships.
- **Blissful productivity:** Gamers are happier when challenged and willing to work hard.
- **Epic meaning:** Gamers like missions and stories and become empowered with hope.

Other research on video gamers is also notable. Brain researcher Jay Pratt investigated what he termed "the useful field of view." That's the ability to see a wider net of activity, or in sports terms, seeing the whole playing field. Women trained on action video games significantly improved the breadth of their field of view. This broader view reveals a dynamic workplace, with many players who impact the ebb and flow of their careers. In other words, it's more than their boss who can help or hurt their advancement.

Although Pratt and McGonigal were studying video gamers, there's a far larger context for their analysis than just the virtual world. This gamer is playing in the real world, in everyday business, in the real time of real lives. Gamesmanship is a way of thinking, and it's an attitude. It uses your inner competitive drive to maximize opportunities. As such, it recognizes that you may lose a round one day, but you can—and will—win one the next day.

To be a great gamer means unleashing your competitive spirit with courage and unbridled enthusiasm in any arena, including the business world. And here, ladies, is where the tension lies.

WHAT WOMEN ARE AND
WHAT WOMEN ARE NOT

Before the enactment of Title IX in 1972, women rarely played college sports. Most in the workplace today were not raised to play team sports growing up, at least not with the intensity afforded the boys. You weren't trained from a young age to learn the importance of mental and physical agility and stamina. You didn't get all of the positive reinforcement that boys got playing games. You didn't hear Fight for it! You go girl! Show 'em what you've got! And that's unfortunate, because *having confidence when you're in the game gives you a better chance of winning at that moment . . . and the next time.* Confidence builds on itself.

And to actually score points, what a euphoric feeling that is!

Things are changing today for the younger generation of women, which is wonderful, but for most of us without such rearing, it's tough to express our competitive spirits outwardly. We like to collaborate, not to compete. Competing requires, by definition, winners and losers. Most women are compassionate; winning, and especially *losing*, requires dispassion. One of the most important teachings of gamesmanship centers on losing. Losing is OK. Losing means you're in the game, you're at least playing, and playing is critical to advancement. The great news is that when you practice the rules in this book, you'll win a whole lot more than you'll lose. The important point is that you're actively a part of the game, and by playing, you're managing your career advancement. In the parlance of games, you can't roll seven if you don't roll the dice.

OH NO, I WON'T BECOME A MAN!

I'm not asking you to. Gamesmanship is one of the languages of business, much like finance. But with any new language, you have to learn how to speak it. Think of it this way: I may want to learn a new language, let's say French. I take lessons, practice, and eventually I'm pretty conversant. If I keep practicing I can even begin to think in French. Does that mean I've lost English as my first language or that I'm any less American? Of course not. Gamesmanship is quite simply another language, a new skill set that will help you become more successful and fulfilled, just like learning a new language.

To keep with the analogy, if France is the business world, it's best if you learn the language to be fluent there. France is populated with the French; business is populated with men. And men have controlled the territory since history began. Until you learn to speak the language of business, men will control the conversation.

You don't forsake any of your womanhood to employ gamesmanship. But, as you will see, I'm asking you to think, and act, more like an athlete. This means showing up with confidence on the playing field and having a winning spirit. It means composure. Mental fortitude. It means loving the game called business and being fueled by the raw adrenaline of winning. *It means thinking like a winner.* With enough practice and use of the steps I outline in this book, you can do this. And I suggest you must, if you want to level the playing field with men. Here's what you're up against.

THE GUYS

My work experience suggests that most men just love to compete. I swear before the alarm clock goes off in the morning they're in bed thinking, Who goes down today? They see much of life, and certainly business, as a game. If you report better profit margins or a better market share than your competitors, it's a win. Outside of business, men think this way too. Case in point: In a November 6, 2012 (Election Day), article in the *Wall Street Journal* titled "For Men, Election Is Like Big Game," a Duke neuroscientist tracked men watching election results and found their hormonal response to be similar to men watching a great ball game with their favorite team on the field.

For those of us who have chosen business as a career, we do have competitive juice. We're not morticians, right? But we tend to focus more on self-mastery than competing with others. There's a name for that—*perfectionism*, which deserves a separate book of its own. This book, however, explains how to channel your drive for self-mastery toward outward competition. There are so many advantages that come from thinking this way. You will get promoted more and move your career along more quickly. You will be able to take loss with grace and to learn from it. You will be better able to coach others, inspiring your team to perform at higher levels as you drive them toward the next win. The excitement is invigorating, and everyone's morale benefits.

The gamer lens also provides the emotional distance you need to win. It helps desensitize you from the politics of corporate life, and it teaches you to set boundaries between work and life. With this lens you will come to understand your male colleagues better and not to personalize so much their interactions with you. Business is a winning game for the men, so shouldn't it be a game for you too? Most important, the gamer lens is a means to level the playing field with men, your constant competitors in the business world.

The best news of all is this: Once you start winning and clear the field from middle management into senior roles, you can influence company cultures from the top down, moving them to become more matriarchal. But first you have to get there.

THE REALITIES FOR WOMEN

Learning good gamesmanship becomes all the more critical because of imbalances women face in the workplace every day. This book doesn't sugarcoat that. If you want a book describing equal standards of behavior in business for women and men, I'd love to write that, but it wouldn't be reality. There is still a wide gender gap, which is why gamesmanship is such an important tool. Let's look at ways women are held to different standards:

♦ In a famous 2003 study by Columbia Business School professor Frank Flynn and New York University professor Cameron Anderson, students were presented with an actual case study of a successful female entrepreneur. Half the students received the case study with the entrepreneur sporting her actual female name. The other half received the same case study with one change: a male name in the entrepreneur spot. The groups gave the businessperson equal marks for respect, but the students whose case study retained the female name were more likely to score the subject as someone who was selfish and not someone they would want to work for. Same data, the only difference being gender.

♦ A Stanford School of Business study on power and influence found that women who are perceived as competent are also often perceived as unlikable. Men, on the other hand, do not face this likability/competency issue.

♦ Behaviors like impulse control are also given a much wider berth for men than women. Men can scream when they're angry. Women can't, if they want to be respected. Men can fool around at work (I've even heard office flings called "sports sex"—ironic given the thesis of this book). Screaming and affairs may generate office chatter, and none of it charitable, but those men won't be relegated to corporate Siberia the way women would. Clearly no one should do either of these things in the workplace, but men often get away with it.

♦ There are words in the business world that are laden with different meanings for men and women. Men can be ambitious, aggressive, and powerful, and that's good. But for women, those same terms can be a negative. A man may be called a boss, and that's a good thing. Even bossy is OK for men; it shows they are in charge. But if a woman is bossy, that's bad. Men are lauded for aggressively pursuing goals. Women who do the same are called pushy. I'll never forget the day my female neighbor, who also had a management job, told me she perceived me as ambitious. You could tell by her tone she didn't mean that as a compliment. My first thought was, She thinks I'm selfish! But then I realized she was right, I *am* ambitious—and that was OK. Perhaps even *we've* been brainwashed to buy into these double standards. Instead of throwing up our hands in frustration, we can play like gamers, and win.

OUR ADVANTAGES

Most women work toward win–win situations. We approach work and life that way, which is why we're such great collaborators and excellent managers of people. The problem with creating win–win situations is that it assumes others around us want win–wins too. What you may find, however, is that often your male teammates prefer a playing field of winners and losers. It's quicker than building consensus, and getting the win is just plain thrilling. It's a real adrenaline high. What can you do about that? Gamesmanship is an excellent solution.

Let's look at all of the advantages women bring to the playing field: a win–win approach to work, intuitive brains, interpersonal skills, strong team management skills, observational and listening skills, an interest in learning, and an impressive work ethic. These attributes have been discussed at length in other books, so in this one I'll focus on new skills to develop and use.

However, there is one advantage listed that is worth a second look—most women are excellent observers and listeners. That ability allows them to get into the heads of their teammates and learn about others in the workplace, be it a colleague, a supervisor, or a client. Once you know people, you can understand what's important to them and how to create win–win situations. But because win–win outcomes are not always possible, Plan B is to beat them good.

Here's a slice-of-life example of why getting into the heads of others seems to come more naturally for women. Have you ever had a conversation with your husband or partner who's just been out with one of the guys? You asked him what went on:

"Nothing," he says.

"How are Jane [wife] and Jimmy [child]?" you ask.

"I don't know. We didn't talk about that."

"Well, what *did* you talk about?"

"Not sure. Not really anything."

Whenever I have these nonconversations with my husband, it reminds me of the joke about the Three Wisewomen, which goes like this. If there had been Three Wisewomen, instead of men, they would have:

+ Asked for directions
+ Arrived on time
+ Helped deliver the baby
+ Cleaned the stable
+ Made a casserole
+ Brought practical gifts

It's a funny reminder that in a broad comparison, men and women are different. It's been that way since we were boys and girls. As a little girl you probably didn't bite your PB&J sandwiches into the shape of a revolver. You didn't punch another girl to say hello. We're just made differently, and this book is not intended to be a male basher. I've learned almost everything I know about business from some very talented men, including gamesmanship. My point in writing is to help other women close the gap and become great gamers too.

TEN RULES OF GAMESMANSHIP

How can you be a gamer? In this book, I'll answer that question with concrete discussion, stories, and solutions. You'll learn the Ten Rules of Gamesmanship and how to use them effectively to succeed.

The first seven rules focus on skills, behaviors, and strategies needed to be a great gamer:

Rule 1: Conditioning
Rule 2: Composure
Rule 3: Playing offense
Rule 4: Brinksmanship strategies
Rule 5: Fan clubs
Rule 6: Practice, practice, practice
Rule 7: Uniform requirements

The last three rules take a holistic approach to gamesmanship through focus on emotional maturity. They round out the process of becoming a business leader.

Rule 8: Good sportsmanship
Rule 9: Grit
Rule 10: Team play

I'll introduce you to each rule, show you how it applies in a business setting, and give you practical ways to incorporate it into your life. At the end of each chapter, in the section titled "Your Turn," I'll summarize the high points and ask that you try the strategies yourself. Many of the rules require a certain finesse because we're women, and I'll point those out too. To become great gamers, you need to sometimes play from the women's tees, or with rules of finesse. It doesn't mean you're not as strong or capable as men; it just means winning at work is often trickier for women than it is for men. For example, the ability to be liked as a leader is a more fragile thing for women, as many feel we're expected to behave in supporting rather than in leading roles.

Along the way, I'll share with you the stories from my own experience as well as the tales of other presidents and CEOs who have become great gamers in their own fields. It's a diverse and rich group of storytellers, and I'm sure you'll learn from them as much as I did when interviewing them.

Business is a team sport. Let's learn how to play.

PART ONE

Chapter 1

It Starts with Conditioning

RULE 1: CONDITIONING

The Game Context: Conditioning is how an athlete goes from good to great. To really succeed on the playing field, you need more than raw talent and enthusiasm. You need physical conditioning and skills. No matter the sport—baseball, gymnastics, soccer—conditioning is a key element to winning.

The Business Setting: Conditioning is how an executive goes from good to great and how you become ready for the corner suite. Smarts, enthusiasm, and ambition will get you only so far. To advance, you must acquire and demonstrate certain technical skills. And skills are not born; they are learned. In this chapter you'll learn three conditioning skills leaders have acquired: line experience, financial knowledge, and a global perspective.

SKILL 1: LINE EXPERIENCE

In 1980, I considered myself one of the luckiest people on the planet. I had landed a job at Home Box Office! There couldn't have been a more glamorous, sexy job out there. As a twenty-five-year-old single woman, I knew I'd hit the jackpot.

True, there were challenges. I didn't anticipate calling on cable operators in Peoria, Illinois, in the arctic dead of winter, or trying to learn the difference between headends and modulators. I was an *advertising* major, for heaven's sake, not some engineer. I had to morph into a faux engineer to do my job, but that's a story for later. Back to the glitz and glamour.

HBO's management had recruited me to do sales in their Midwest territory. I enjoyed the work and was rewarded with several promotions. But even in my happy state, I could look around the organization and see there were others out there having even more fun than I was. There was a woman who ran PR for the Midwest—Karen. She traveled with the stars, got to go to Hollywood premieres, and overall appeared to have a marvelous time doing a lot of schmoozing. I decided I wanted that job.

When Karen left, the job was vacant. I was working under the regional vice president, Bill Grumbles, and marched right into his office. "Bill," I started, "I was thinking I could do Karen's job really well. Now that's she gone, I'd be a great candidate. What do you think?"

Bill paused. "Susan, do you want to run a company someday?"

I hadn't really thought *quite* that far ahead, being twenty-five. But Bill had. "Sure," I replied.

"Then don't you dare consider a PR job. That only supports your important work in sales to bring in revenue. Sales is line work. Line work will get you a big job someday."

Bill gave me my first lesson in line vs. support jobs, which was a game-changer for me. It was my first lesson in the power-building process of conditioning.

Line vs. Support Jobs

The term *line job*, also referred to as an operating job, comes from the military language around line soldiers. These are the guys who serve on the front lines of battle, taking the risks and getting decorated and promoted, or dying if they fail. In short, line jobs are the combat positions of the business world.

People holding line jobs are found at all levels of the corporate hierarchy. They are general managers, sales reps, and division heads. They are the ones whose jobs and functions are clearly tied to revenue and profit generation. In sports like soccer, the front lines score the points for a team. The same is true in business. Line people score, or increase, business for the company. The risks and rewards of a line job are clear. You live and die by your results, and executing with speed and a sense of urgency is required. In this way line jobs share the gamer trait of *urgent optimism*. Line managers see excitement and promise in their job initiatives and have a relentless focus on execution. If you fail to deliver, you can expect your compensation to be at risk. On the flip side, if you are successful, you can expect bonuses, raises, and other benefits to come your way because these jobs move the needle at a company.

Raises and bonuses are great, but I loved line work because that's where all the action is. You can see the results of your work. Jobs like sales, product development, and many others that directly impact the profit and loss of a company give you an instant report card. You can drive a company's success in these jobs, even if you are not CEO. Line jobs are primary to a company's mission; the rest support, and thus are called support jobs.

What is line and what is support is not always clear. Marketing positions, for example, help to generate demand for products and services, but that work is not easily quantifiable, so it falls into a gray zone. Sometimes chief marketing officers make it to the corner office, but they usually have other skill sets under their belt, like sales experience, to get there. Legal officers may be direct reports to a CEO, but their job is support to the rest of the organization. They do not generate profits or directly impact a company's profits and losses (P&L), so while that person may be highly situated in an organization, she or he is considered support.

Line jobs are great conditioning because they teach and build the valuable art of directly impacting profit generation. It's training to make you a leader.

Some Unlikely Line Jobs

One can occupy line positions in the most unlikely of places. While this book deals primarily with business, you may be passionate about working in another sector, such as athletics. (Here I go again with athletics and its parallels to business, but there really are so many it's hard to overlook the overlaps.) I could find no one better to talk to about this than Joan Cronan. As I mentioned earlier, Joan reached the pinnacle of success as a businesswoman in the world of athletics. She was the women's athletic director for the University of Tennessee for thirty years, and in 2011, she was named athletic director for both men's and women's athletics there. No other woman had ever held that position in the SEC.

Anyone who knows anything about college athletics knows about the SEC. This isn't some prissy, beleaguered conference that you never hear about. This is Alabama, Florida, Georgia, South Carolina, Auburn, and other powerhouse sports programs. The SEC is *the* top conference in the country for football, and football generates the most revenue for college sports.

It's easy to tell that a job like Joan's is line and not support by looking at what must be done each day: It's a to-do list full of revenue drivers, all wrapped up in collegiate sports finery. As she described it: "I use the three F's that you have to have in our business. You have to know finance, you have to know football, and you have to know fund-raising. If you don't know these three in the world I live in, you're not going to rise to the top."

Like any good businessperson, she looked at her portfolio of projects, each discrete but together rolling up to one big bottom line. She approached the process like any businessperson does when developing initiatives that will be money losers for a time, supported by the big profit generators.

We have twenty-one sports at the University of Tennessee. Technically we have three businesses and eighteen charities, because you have football and men's and women's basketball that make money, and you have to balance that with all of these other sports that are just as important, but they don't have the potential of making the revenue of football or men's and women's basketball.

UT's program of women's basketball, coached by the winningest coach of all time, Pat Summitt, was part of Joan's portfolio. Very few women's basketball programs make money, but UT's does. Pat worked for Joan, and together they transformed the sport of basketball for young women everywhere, and they did it by seeing sports as a line job. Over a period of three decades at the university, they unleashed their competitive juice and made the young women's sport a winner for UT.

Let's look at other work in the traditional business world that one might not regard as line but surely is—what I like to call the intrapreneur. This is someone who may be working for a big company but functioning as a line player by scouting new opportunities for revenue. Dean Gilbert has played that role many times. He is a lifelong friend of mine; we met in graduate school and have stayed close over the years of our careers. Dean grew up on the "disruptive" side of media and distribution, meaning the new, emerging forms of media, technology, and distribution that would alter, or disrupt, consumer habits. He got into the cable TV business early during the go-go years. He was involved when pagers were exploding and from there, the beginnings of cell phones. He quickly pivoted to the high-speed Internet industry, became a founding general manager of a very successful Silicon Valley baby called @Home, and ultimately joined Google. Before he departed Google, he was running all content and operations for YouTube. Both he and I share a love for invention and for finding growth opportunities even within big companies. It's called being an intrapreneur, or an entrepreneur within an established (translation: profitable) company. Intrapreneurial jobs push a company's growth trajectory dramatically. Dean says:

> *If you start your career in larger companies or in more traditional, more mature industries, try to look for those intrapreneurial opportunities. Don't just focus on the part of the business that's the big, thick, mature beast. I always was looking for that next thing,*

even when I was in a company that was more of a traditional type. There were always new products and new services, new ideas, and I tended to always migrate to the things that were the new thing. That really helped me to prepare to run a company or be a part of a startup.

This was true in my career too. The first company I worked for, HBO, was originally a small promising business under the enormous Time Inc. parent. I started there when VCRs were just coming of age in the early 1980s, and we worked through strategies to ward off the competition. Fascinating stuff at the time. We created new brands, like Cinemax and Festival, a precursor to HBO Family, to protect our big brand HBO. Some of these made it; others did not. When I joined NBC a few years later, I was part of the startup team for a completely new sector called cable programming, and I helped to launch and grow CNBC. At Scripps Networks, I was on the ground floor of HGTV. When it turned profitable, and our acquisition Food Network was also turning profitable, I moved to head up a new business unit called New Ventures. Our goal was to incubate new brands and platforms. I loved this work. My contributions in these areas pushed the company into new sources of growth, making them definitively line positions.

Play to Win

A 2012 study by consulting firm McKinsey & Company found that line management experience plays a key role in the successful advancement of female executives. But while many women in top positions credit their line management experience for their success, too few women coming up in the ranks are getting that line job training. I'm far from an expert on why women often choose support jobs over line work, but I suspect it's a combination of many things: the risk, the need to make a reliable income, the safety with what is known. We will talk with Ronee Hagen, former CEO of Polymer Group, in more detail later in this chapter. But to this particular point, when I asked her about why women choose certain career tracks over others, she left me with something to ponder. She asked, "Susan, why do we [women] play not to lose, versus playing to win?" Hmm, that's a very good question, ladies.

If you want to run a company someday or operate in senior roles, you need experience with line jobs. They're where the excitement and the rewards lie. They are the rock 'n' roll of business. Conditioning, or skill building, in this area is critical for future success.

SKILL 2: FINANCE KNOWLEDGE

In grade school I made my way like most little girls of my time, terrified of math and loving English. In ninth grade I had a math teacher named Mr. Barr whose job it was to teach us simple algebra. My two best friends, Chris and Michelle, were girl anomalies because math was a breeze for them, and they loved it. The first day we sat in Mr. Barr's room they were beaming, and I was quivering.

I ended up doing well, albeit with an unorthodox approach. In my own mental process, I needed to eliminate all of the answers it couldn't possibly be before I got to the right one. Unlike Chris and Michelle, who thought in a clear, linear way, let's just say my thinking was a bit . . . circuitous. In the beginning, Mr. Barr couldn't quite believe it, so he'd call on me to solve for x up at the chalkboard. As I illustrated my answers to homework problems, my solutions could take a full chalkboard of x's and y's. Recall, this was *simple* algebra. Later in life, I would learn to get to the point much more quickly. And I would learn the importance of being comfortable with numbers if I wanted to run a company.

Scorecards

Let's start with budgets. At some point in your business career you will be responsible for one. Simply put, you will be allotted a portion of your company's capital to manage. Your care and feeding of the budget, so to speak, will earn you favor if managed prudently.

Think of it like your allowance. It's yours—how will you best spend it? If you blow it on a new pair of shoes, you won't have anything left over for the rest of the outfit.

As you advance into executive management, you will get exposed to income statements. You need to learn how to interpret them so you can know what's going on in the overall company. In their most simplistic form, income statements express a company's revenues, expenses, and (we hope) profits. Revenues minus expenses equals profit. I am dramatically oversimplifying here, but the fundamental purpose of these reports is to track how much money your company is making. Income statements are the company's scorecard.

Since I took absolutely zero business or finance classes in college, income statements and balance sheets were completely foreign to me. While at CNBC I asked NBC's management to send me somewhere to learn some finance. They agreed, and I was sent to a two-week program at the University of Virginia (UVA) in Charlottesville, which was run by the Darden School of Business.

I quickly discovered there was something in Charlottesville other than boring numbers and intimidating finance professors. There was Monticello, home of Thomas Jefferson. After spending a couple of afternoons there gathering newfound kernels of history, and practicing avoidance behavior, I knew I'd flunk out if I didn't go to class. I found a couple of novice students in the class like me, and we became a study team. I passed with their help, and the short course set me on a path of understanding what was needed to run a company someday. The knowledge came in very handy when I was made chief operating officer of HGTV and needed to meet with our shareholders.

Finance is a business language. If you understand and can speak it, you will know how to communicate the financial health of your company to others.

Financial vs. Accounting Knowledge

We return now to Ronee Hagen, whom we met briefly earlier in this chapter. When I interviewed her, she was getting ready to retire from being CEO of Polymer Group, a multibillion-dollar company specializing in consumer and industrial goods. Ronee made a profound point about the difference between financial vs. accounting knowledge: "I think the grounding that is important for leadership is to really understand the difference between the economic decisions in business and . . . what are just SEC accounting rules that have nothing to do with running the business. Some people can either be intimidated or be diverted or confused by the distinction."

Unless you're CFO or otherwise in the accounting department of a company, you don't need to understand the rules of accounting. Issues around reporting practices, commonly accepted principles handed down by the SEC, what can be written off, what should be capitalized, if and when a company you're acquiring will be accretive—you can leave the technical reporting for your financial people. Sure, it helps to know it, but it's not vital. A good CFO is invaluable to you because she knows all these things.

What you *do* need to understand are the metrics that drive the financial performance of your company and industry. You need to know how much cash your company has and how much debt you are carrying. Looking at your income statement, you need to know what kind of margins you have compared your industry competitors so you can kill them on a daily basis. You need to know how much your company is worth by outside metrics, such as multiples of earnings, so you can track your growth and know the value of what you and your team are building. (Earnings multiples are a financial formula that projects future earnings and pegs your company's value to a potential buyer.) Such knowledge also helps you make the proper economic decisions as a leader of your company: Should you invest in a new process, building, or company? Why are your revenues lagging from last quarter or last month? What's the cause of this spike on the research or marketing expense line? Good executives are in enough meetings with their folks to know, almost intuitively, the economic health and vitality of their organizations, without needing constant study of their scorecard. But income statements are important reference tools, and if you're a publicly traded company, you have a responsibility to your shareholders to know your scorecard in and out. Trust me, your investors will ask.

Public Companies

This section is aimed at those of you who work for public companies, but it offers valuable knowledge for anyone in a business setting.

Publicly traded companies have quarterly calls or meetings in which they release their results. Investors will ask about any number of things, including the metrics that are customarily used in your industry. When I was HGTV's COO, one of my key duties was distribution. My job, and that of my distribution team, was to sell HGTV to cable operators and satellite providers, who would then transmit the network into viewer homes. Every viewer who received HGTV was called a subscriber. The investors would grill me about how many subscribers we had, how many would be rolling out from new deals, time lines, and the like. They did this because they had a formula, which said these subscribers were worth $10 each. I have no idea where that formula originated, but when a network like ours was still losing money, the financials hung on how many subscribers you had, which investors could then translate into the intrinsic value of the business. Once we turned profitable, they looked at multiples of cash flow and enterprise value and earnings. Each company has its own key metrics that investors will want to dissect. You must be knowledgeable about them if you are in these meetings.

The Dow

When I was back in graduate school about a million years ago getting a master's degree in advertising, there was a married couple in the program. I'll call them The Couple because I can't recall their names. They were nice enough, but it sure seemed they had no social life outside of themselves and school. I had no problem having a social life outside of school, if you get my drift. When we were close to graduating, we all began interviewing for jobs. The Couple was always a step or two ahead of the rest of us in getting the interviews and certainly in getting job offers. One day, they were replaying for us a more challenging interview they had each had (who knows, maybe they interviewed as a package). But no problem, they aced it. The ad agency interviewer had asked if they knew what the Dow Jones represented, and what the current Dow Jones average was that day. "Twelve hundred," one of them replied with a smug smile. Meanwhile, I was thinking, *The Dow? WTF?*

The Couple actually helped me a great deal. I went home and learned all about the Dow, because heaven forbid it would come up in one of my interviews and I wouldn't be prepared (it never did). This conditioning greatly helped me when I went to work at CNBC, because the network's mission was to be a knowledgeable money manager for those watching the channel. Follow the Dow and the S&P if you work in a publicly traded company. They are important indicators of the overall financial health of the economy.

Summing It Up

Getting to be comfortable with the language of numbers is a critical skill set for executive management. I learned it on the job, through continuing education, and by asking others for help. Even with the education I got, I still carried around a little cheat sheet of financial terms and their definitions, such as the difference between *cash flow* and *free cash flow* and other terms that investors would banter around on our quarterly calls. I met with my CFO constantly to continue my education. To be an effective leader, you can never stop learning or asking others for help.

One of our most visible female leaders agrees. In Supreme Court Justice Sonia Sotomayor's 2013 book, *My Beloved World*, she says she has asked others for their wisdom throughout her life. She recounts a time in grade school when she learned from another girl how to study:

The most critical lesson I learned that day is still one too many kids never figure out: don't be shy about making a teacher of any willing party who knows what he or she is doing. In retrospect, I can see how important that pattern would become for me, how readily I've sought out mentors, asking guidance from professors or colleagues, and in every friendship soaking up early whatever that friend could teach me.

For someone who thought the Dow was a cleaning product, I'm living proof you can learn enough about finance to be informed, well-reasoned, and dangerous to your competition.

SKILL 3: A GLOBAL PERSPECTIVE

You can't consider your conditioning complete until you've taken the practice to a global level. You may be acquiring all the skills to compete at home, but do you have the skills to compete *anywhere*? True conditioning builds the skills necessary to win on any stage.

In September 2012, I sat in London's Landmark hotel having lunch with some friends and colleagues from the Committee of 200 (C200), a group of the world's most senior women business leaders. Most of us are from the United States, but we also have members from England, Germany, Japan, Kuwait, Switzerland, Colombia, Sweden, and Africa. I was in London to participate in an outreach event, which is where we visit universities and mentor women who are in business programs. I have been to Europe, South Africa, Botswana, and many U.S. locations for outreach efforts. We offer scholarships as well as our time, mentoring, and advocacy.

This particular afternoon, an impressive array of women sat

around me. There was Sylvie Grégoire, former president of Shire Human Genetic Therapies; Tanya Fratto, former General Electric executive and Boart Longyear board member; Herta von Stiegel, chief executive officer of Ariya Capital; Marisa Drew, co-head of EMEA's investment banking department and global co-head of Global Market Solutions, Credit Suisse; Donna Couch, owner and principal of Couch Consultants and former ExxonMobil executive; Roz Alford, principal at ASAP; Dorrit Bern, former chairman and chief executive officer of Charming Shoppes; and Ruth M. Owades, founder of several gardening companies that have been used as Harvard case studies. We were preparing to address the women from the London Business School. Of those who were with me at lunch, more than half currently worked somewhere other than the Americas. Many had transferred to jobs in Europe and Africa. One woman moved eight times around the world for different assignments. They shared how living and working overseas had greatly enhanced their skill base and their breadth of perspective as well as preparing them for senior roles in corporate America.

This is what a global view is all about: learning that the rest of the world is an enormous, dynamic collection of cultures and economies that you can profit from, both economically and intellectually. A global view is about recognizing that the good ole U.S. of A. is today a dominant economy but that it is increasingly dependent on the rest of the world to sustain and grow it; understanding that even if your business may be local, your competition is likely owned by a company that's a multinational entity; and remembering that most of the world's customers live outside our domestic borders.

As I listened to my C200 colleagues reflect on their career experiences at lunch that day, I thought about the work I had done in Canada and then later in the rest of the world. I didn't have the experience of living overseas, but I did build global businesses from my U.S. perch at both CNBC and HGTV. At CNBC, we had purchased the assets of a failed channel called the Financial News Network (FNN). One thing the FNN management did right was to seize an opportunity to get distributed in Canada. When NBC purchased FNN, it was my job to retain that foothold as we converted FNN into CNBC.

Some dismiss Canada as not being an important strategic foothold, given it shares our borders, *and they speak English*. When I hear that, I point out that Canada is our largest trading partner in the world—although China is closing in fast—so yes, it matters. For media companies it's very tough to do business in Canada because of those shared borders, as the government is wary of its culture being hijacked by U.S. media influences. I successfully converted the dying FNN channel into CNBC because the Canadian regulators, called the Canadian Radio-Television and Telecommunications Commission (CRTC), had no other option for financial news at the time, and they'd grown dependent on FNN's information.

It wasn't nearly as easy when I later worked in Canada with HGTV.

As we were in the first year of trying to get HGTV off the ground in the States, I recognized that opportunities for U.S. media companies in Canada were closing. I convinced my CEO and the other founders that we needed to get in there quickly with HGTV, even though we had our hands more than full with our domestic agenda. Timing is everything with international work; you can strike too fast and lose a boatload of money, or you can wait too long and be closed out. In the late 1980s and early 1990s, the Weather Channel and the Travel Channel tried to gain footholds in Europe and lost millions. They were there too early with aggressive strategies and didn't test the prudence of their plans before they made their offensive play. Megabrand ESPN had to pull out of the UK after losing some sports rights to local companies. Even for a powerhouse U.S. company, there are many challenges to becoming a winning global brand.

Partners

To do business successfully overseas, local relationships are critical. Local partners are especially critical for media companies because foreign leadership wants to safeguard its culture and mores, and media is one of the largest expressions of them. Importing American media can be threatening. With my CNBC experience I had built relationships in Canada, which proved to be very helpful for HGTV. I knew we needed a strong partner in order to attain approval. I chose a great group, Alliance Atlantis, and we petitioned the CRTC to get approval for a joint partnership of Alliance Atlantis/Scripps and to launch a home-and-garden lifestyle channel in Canada.

The experience of working with foreign governments is greatly rewarding but can be downright intimidating if you don't have your A-game going. The rules of gamesmanship are in full roar here. You need to know the answers to certain questions, such as: What does this government want to win? Is it possible to have us both win through some strategic game play and compromise? What does the big win look like for my company?

I had many discussions with my CEO to be sure we were on the same page regarding these questions. I then journeyed to Toronto and spent a full weekend with Alliance Atlantis doing role-plays, in preparation for petitioning the CRTC to gain access. I loved that we were doing this, because it reflected a shared sense of how the rules of gamesmanship could help us to win our petition. One of my partners played the role of commissioner and fired questions at me that, through practice, I smoothly answered. We prepared for our big meeting the following Monday with the gamer rule of practice, practice, practice. We conditioned ourselves to be ready for anything. But none of us could have ever predicted that the first question directed at me would be, "In your content description, Ms. Packard, you mention home electronics as a part of your program offering in the United States. What do you mean by that?"

Back in the States, we had an original content description that included home electronics, which we had failed to update over time. Home electronics hadn't been on any programming grid I'd seen lately. Did this commissioner love the idea of home electronics or hate it? Had he just installed a home theater and was buzzing about it? Which chess move should I make here? I looked at my partner and spoke. "Well, in the States, we had discussed some shows that might include home electronics, and while these ideas have not been fleshed out there, here in Canada, together with our respected partner, we might produce some shows that would include these themes."

The key words were *together*—yes, we would work closely with our partner—and *might*, since I worried that these concepts might not be viable. A lesson learned in that meeting was that no matter how much you practice and role-play, there are often elements of surprise in the game. This is when, no matter how much conditioning you've done, composure and agility, some of our other gamer tactics, need to kick in.

We won the petition, and today have a thriving Canadian channel, along with partners who contribute greatly to its success.

After that experience I began to create an international department, and with the help of a small but mighty team, led by Kristen

Jordan, we expanded all over the world. In English-speaking countries we pursued full channels, and in the rest of the world we sold shows or branded blocks of our content. When I departed in the summer of 2010, we had a presence in over 170 countries. Today SNI is in over 200 countries and translated in twenty-three languages for viewers.

How and Why Choose Global Work?

Global assignments are the conditioning that will teach you to succeed in the borderless business world. There are many ways to get involved with international work. If your company is just beginning to expand internationally, determine what you can bring to the table, then request a seat at it. If you have a finance background, excellent. Finance minds are always needed to make sure the business will build to help, not damage, the overall P&L. If you have an operations background, there will be work needed on uplinks, satellite feeds, and shipping content in various languages. It's also easier to be considered for an international assignment if you are fluent in the language of the target country.

If your company is up and running with international operations already in place, strategize what you might contribute to these operations. Are you willing to relocate and become one of the feet on the ground in some other part of the world? Are you willing to travel extensively to serve in some capacity from the States? Begin with what your skill base is, and think about how it can help the overseas business. There are plenty of resources you can tap too. I list some at the chapter's end.

Why bother? The pragmatic answer is that those with global experience are better equipped to run a company someday. Most of the Fortune 500 companies have active international operations. They're the promised land of new growth and revenues. You can't read a business story today without some reference to China, India, or Brazil and many other growing economies. Case in point: Yahoo!'s core business is crumbling, but investors still like it because of its holdings in China, where it has substantial interest in China's hot Internet site called Alibaba.

Here's the better answer, in my view. It's what we learn from our work overseas that makes us better people and better citizens. It's an opening to new vistas of all kinds. We learn the true meaning of partnership, since we depend on good partners to guide us in the most appropriate uses of our assets. We learn the importance of trust. Of course, there is plenty of formal vetting that goes on with picking partners, but at the end of the day, we have to make some untested judgments on the partners to whom we entrust our brands and other assets.

We also learn the importance of cross-cultural collaboration, of working with diverse teams, of tolerance and respect. CEOs like Starbucks's Howard Schultz understand this, and in 2013 he organized meetings in Beijing and Shanghai with the *parents* of his Chinese employees. He felt it was important to let the parents know what Starbucks stood for to those who have, in his words a "unique relationship to the one child" they have birthed. By working abroad we gain respect and humility when we see how interdependent our world really is. Many of these reasons underlie the study abroad programs at universities, and if you've ever spoken with students who've returned from one of these, most come away feeling enriched. A friend and mentor once said that global study and global work are like getting a "world life degree."

From a management perspective, working globally enriches your company culture. It adds more diversity, more points of view, more learning for your workforce. More fun too. I recently visited my old stomping ground, SNI, and some employees of Indian descent had brought in foods from their native land for colleagues to try during lunchtime.

In my son's high school in Knoxville, Tennessee, a town of less than 200,000 people, they are teaching Mandarin now, along with Spanish, French, and German. The world is much bigger than our borders. We come to learn and appreciate its richness when we develop a worldview—or, in keeping with sports metaphor, a view from the blimp.

I started this book with the chapter on conditioning because these conditioning skills prepare you for the biggest stage, that of CEO. Even if your career goals are more modest, say, middle management work, learning at least one of these skills will make you more qualified for advancement, when the time is right for you. It all starts with conditioning.

YOUR TURN

Line Experience (see page 219)

1. Ask yourself, Do I want to run a company someday or become a senior leader? If yes, look for opportunities in line work.
2. Moving to line work may mean you need to pivot into other departments within your company. Learn what background is needed to move into those jobs.
3. Seek out line supervisors in your target area and express your interest. Show commitment by being willing to get some additional schooling or technical skills.

Finance Knowledge

4. If your company is publicly traded, your income statements are readily available. Go to your company's website, click on the investor relations link, and you should find them there.

5. Take someone from the accounting department to lunch. Ask for a lesson in how to understand your company's income statement. Accounting folks love to talk numbers if you are truly interested.

6. Don't be shy about carrying cheat sheets, which define the finance terms that may be new to you. You are learning a new language. No one expects you to be fluent at the start.

7. Take a class at your local community college or university to learn finance. Then take your friend from accounting to lunch and show 'em what you know! Continue to cultivate this relationship and meet every few months to brush up on your company's scorecard.

A Global Perspective (see page 220)

8. Be willing to learn a second language, or if you speak another language, be sure your global managers know this as you express your interest in international work.

9. Determine how your skill sets can match up with the global work—what value you can add—then make your pitch.

10. Always be respectful of the cultures you are working in. This also means learning many of their behaviors, such as how to greet and to depart meetings respectfully, and food choices as well as dining etiquette. Books abound that can inform you on the customs of various cultures.

Chapter 2

Play It Cool

RULE 2: COMPOSURE

The Game Context: While you rarely hear the term *composure* used in game discussions, it has plenty of applications. As Tom Hanks's character so famously said in *A League of Their Own*, "There's no crying in baseball." On the playing field, winners are those who maintain composure even if they're facing a loss. The player on the field screaming at the ref over a bad call, calling his fellow players out for a mistake, visibly losing it, is not the guy who is inspiring confidence. In fact, that loss of composure may well be a sign that he's a weak link on the team.

The Business Setting: Respect and promotions in the workplace go to the individual who has a calm and confident presence, whether it's in one-on-one meetings, in team settings, or in commanding a room. Composure shows you're grounded and in control of your emotions. It communicates to your colleagues that you make rational, well-reasoned decisions. It is an important leadership quality.

THERE'S NOTHING LIKE COOL

Mariano Rivera is known as the greatest baseball closer of all time.

If you don't know baseball, the closer comes into the game in the last inning to "close out," or complete a team's win. He's the last man the opposing team faces, if all goes well, and he shuts out the side. This job requires mental fortitude like few others. Everything is on the line.

Rivera retired in the fall of 2013 from the New York Yankees, where he celebrated a career like no other closer. Jason Gay of the *Wall Street Journal* wrote an article about him during this time titled "Let's Be Cool Like Mariano Rivera." He wrote of Mariano's grace, dignity, and restraint. Gay yearned for Rivera's cool, which he says he'll never have. "I drop a bagel on the subway and I want to call 911." And since I can't say it better than he did, here are Gay's words:

> *If I could pick one thing to steal from Mariano Rivera—what would be more useful than anything else—it's his cool. Mariano Rivera is as cool as it gets in sports. The right, proper cool. Not the manufactured, phony cool that they try to give you with a soft-drink commercial. . . . Authentic cool. Smooth cool. Paul Newman cool. . . . He gets to work. He keeps the job simple, calm, level-headed. Never too emotionally high. Never too low. Powers through a line-up like he's shaving before work.*

Gay doesn't use the word, but Rivera displays the trait I'll talk about in this chapter—*composure*. It's the one that is necessary to win a game, on the field or in the boardroom.

COMPOSURE: WHY AND HOW?

To be a successful gamer, you need to carry yourself with composure. It's not about being an automaton. It's about how you handle yourself so that you can command the room. Those in leadership roles are most effective when they maintain their composure, because the troops know they can count on a level-headed leader to make well-reasoned decisions. As a composed leader, you are constantly reinforcing to your team that you are making stable, consistent decisions.

Many of the female CEOs I interviewed for this book underscored the importance of composure. Ronee Hagen said she never got too emotionally distraught about business. To her she just saw it as a wonderful game. Amy Miles, CEO of Regal Entertainment, the largest owner of movie theater chains in the United States, said that when she sensed her team was stressed, she'd remind them they were just selling popcorn and showing movies—it wasn't heart surgery.

Everyone who works for you is paying attention, especially because women are still in the minority running businesses. Women are being watched and evaluated all the time. Margaret Thatcher, one of the first major female political leaders in the West, was scrutinized from all angles—including her composure—like no male politician before her. When the media praised Germany's Angela Merkel for her handling of the euro debt crisis, stories pointed out her "impassive, no-drama demeanor" as one of her key skills. Well, you might not be a prime minister of the free world, but as a female business leader, your composure and carriage are subject to nonstop scrutiny too.

It's a common stereotype that women are too emotional to handle leadership roles. When a woman is in command, naysayers will be watching for her to make emotional decisions rather than strategic ones. If she yells, or appears rattled, or (heaven forbid) cries, her detractors will pounce. Never mind that Tiger Woods curses like a sailor when he misses a putt or Speaker of the House John Boehner cries in public on a regular basis. For women, the composure standard is different.

Then there's the gamer reason to keep your cool: If you lose your head, it can cost you the game. You appear weak. You cede control to another when he sees you in a position of vulnerability, which is especially important to avoid as you compete for promotions and plum assignments. When you are debating or persuading and you keep your head, you appear in control to all around you.

In this chapter I'll look first at composure and then at how your speech patterns impact your persona. I'll end by providing some self-care tips to help you keep your cool at work.

Early Training

I had my first real brush with needing composure in fairly extreme circumstances. While at HBO I called on a cable system in the Northeast. When I was escorted into the client's office, he pointed me to a chair. The chair was bolted down, and about half the length of a football field from the client's desk, where he was sitting. That was strange enough, but after he shook my hand, he walked over to a rifle case behind me. He pulled one rifle out of the case, walked over, and pointed it at me.

"Do you shoot?" he asked, as the barrel of the rifle was exactly flush with my forehead.

"Uh . . . no, no, I don't," I murmured. "I assume you do?"

He then set down the rifle and launched into his hunting exploits.

It was a very uncomfortable moment, and it was clearly a test. I passed. I stayed calm (likely because I was frozen in fear). I was able to move the conversation in a different direction by focusing on the placards gracing his walls, showing his accomplishments in the cable business. Eventually we came around to discussion of HBO. I got that business because I kept my composure. He was checking to see if I could do it.

Having composure really is doable. I was not born with the composure that got me through meetings at gunpoint. As a child, I had the nickname Sensitive Sue. It was not hard to get me to cry. I am naturally very expressive and can impulsively speak my mind. (It's hard to be Italian and Greek without being expressive.) Growing up, I could slip right into being the Princess of Drama. In high school I was in all the school plays and loved acting out parts—on stage and off. And just as a matter of course, I tend to move quickly. These are not traits that encourage composure. *All* of this had to be reined in as I rose into the executive ranks.

This brings me to a very important point in gamesmanship: Remember that in business we are playing a grand game. Sometimes it requires us to be acting a part, even if we don't feel it. I've had to lead company rallies around reaching goals plenty of times when I didn't feel it because I was distracted with other work issues. It was illuminating to watch Mary Barra, CEO at General Motors, cheering on her thousands of employees to keep pushing and performing in the midst of devastating recalls that gripped her company. We play roles in business all the time. We still suit up and show up as leaders.

The same goes with composure. Sometimes, in a new situation where there's a lot on the line, you may be so tense inside you have to unlock your jaw to speak. What matters is that the words come out. No one else knows how you feel or what you're thinking if you *act* cool. Plenty of your colleagues have jitters too; it's a completely natural way to feel. Acting composed is as effective as truly being composed.

Watch the Pros Work

Watch some successful people. Many of them model the ABC's of composure all the time.

Consider Richard Branson, the successful and flamboyant founder of Virgin Group. He also advocates composure—for him this means putting the brakes on workplace aggression. Virgin is successful in part because the company advocates a climate of positive and inclusive engagement. Aggression—the combative, negative kind—is frowned upon. He acknowledges that this isn't always easy. But maintaining a positive approach is a personal and corporate value. Richard offers a great example of composure, the kind that keeps negative feelings in check and allows positive ones to rule the day.

Composure can often be a subtle thing. I worked for a man early in my career who had a sly way of being cool. Frank Biondi was one of three HBO presidents, which was a strange leadership structure, especially so because of the fierce competition among the three men. Frank's presentation style was unique. The first time I noticed it, he strolled, cool and contained, into a sales meeting where I sat in the audience. He got his slides up on the screen and began with a disclaimer to "Bear with me, it's the first time I've seen these slides." I thought, Wow, busy man, ya know? He was masterful in walking through them. I was very impressed.

The next time he presented to the sales team he began with the same disclaimer, "Bear with me, this is my first time seeing these slides." This was fishy. He just couldn't be *that* busy or, worse yet, that disorganized to not prepare.

Then it dawned on me; he was playing us. Gaming us. His move was for us to admire his mastery of the subject matter, ergo his brilliance, cool and calm, without any prep. It was a display of composure—albeit a setup on his part. These were his rules, and it probably worked for a lot of people he was in the game with.

A Sports Pro

Mike Krzyzewski is the men's basketball coach of the Duke University Blue Devils and one of the winningest college coaches. He has a mantra he refers to as "next play." When his basketball team goes up and down the court and completes a play he yells, "Next play!," meaning don't dwell on what just happened, good or bad. Nothing is so important that it requires a lot of energy to celebrate or tear apart. It's a way to keep his team's head in the game. Keep moving, keep going, next play. Stay cool, and keep your head in the game.

BODY LANGUAGE: TEARS AND EXPRESSIONS

Your physical presence is a manifestation of your composure, whether you realize it or not. Your eyes, your face, your stance, even the way you sit in a meeting—all are barometers for the composure you feel and display to others.

Tears

Some of us tear up easily. It could be due to our genes or our rearing. It doesn't really matter. Sometimes tears are understandable. I lived through a work crisis where my colleague committed suicide after murdering his wife. I cried hard; the whole team did. Later in my career, my mother and my sister, Linda, died unexpectedly in a span of thirty days. These are life events that emotionally level us. When I was in a meeting and found myself drifting back to my mom and Linda, I would excuse myself from the meeting to take a bathroom break.

Women don't cry in business, says style doyenne Martha Stewart. On an episode of the reality show spinoff *The Apprentice: Martha Stewart*, Martha confronted an emotional female contestant. Women in business don't cry, Martha told her. If you do, she promised, you're finished.

Facial Expressions

Often women I work with will say, "Why do they think I'm a bitch and mean-spirited, when I'm not?" Unless you're looking in the mirror a lot—and granted, some of us do—your facial expressions at work are probably not something you pay much attention to. But you should. Facial language, like body language, conveys all kinds of messaging. There's "tough face," which women often don without even realizing it. It signals "stay away." You may walk into a meeting with a tough face. It may be your facial default mechanism, and it can lead others to view you as negative and off-putting. The best thing to do—as silly as this may sound—is to practice smiling in the mirror. Not goofy grins, but a pleasant face that will be inviting to others. Some friends and I were at a conference recently where this was discussed, and my friend Sherri Lee leaned over to me. She noted that she is always conscious of entering a room with a smile. Now that she's sixtyish, her face pulls downward without a little help propping it up. So she uses those smile muscles a lot.

Composure is not just about facial expressions. It's also about full body language. How do you carry yourself in the workplace? Do you sit up straight in meetings and lean in to the discussion? Do you stand tall when presenting? Are you in the center of the space or are you edging off to the side? When in a difficult meeting, do you cross your arms and legs defensively or do you sit in a relaxed but professional stance to convey your ease? Silent or speaking, your body language is communicating. And you want it to say, I am composed (even when you don't really feel that way). Your goal in your body language is to invite others in, not make them uncomfortable or, worse, scare them off.

Now let's turn to how we speak, which can get us into as much trouble as how we carry ourselves.

ALL THOSE WORDS!

Composure isn't just physical; it is also verbal. And many women aren't aware of this.

Boston Consulting Group reported that women speak about 20,000 words a day, while men average about 7,000. Women are less inclined to "get to the period" than men. It's a little bit nature and a little bit nurture and a lot due to stress. Under stressful situations women can tend to babble on. This can be off-putting on a playing field of men. Women's language is often full of tentative expressions and disclaimers before beginning a sentence, such as, "I believe," "I think," "I'm pretty sure that," and similar precursors to making a point. Some start and end sentences with *sorry*—sorry for bothering you; sorry this issue has come up; sorry, sorry, sorry. Then there's the "I could be wrong but," which is the worst of all. If you begin to pay attention to how you speak, you may find these patterns. They are useless, empty words that serve to weaken your point and reflect a lack of conviction. Beware of them.

Men *do not* like a lot of words. The simpler and the clearer, the better. Pat Mitchell, who started out in teaching and eventually rose to be CEO of PBS and, most recently, retired president of New York's Paley Center for Media, recounts her first meeting with media mogul Ted Turner:

> *The first meeting I had with Ted he cut me off after about three sentences. And I thought, wait a minute, I'm not through, I did all this work, I've got all this preparation done, I'm ready to tell you more. And he said, "I'm not ready to hear it, meeting over." I was so upset. I went back to my office and was writing my resignation letter because I was thinking, I am forty-something years old, I've been in this business twenty years, and I'm not going to have somebody just say no. Then he called me on the phone. He said, "I know you're upset; why are you so upset?" I said, "Because nobody since my father told me no when they didn't have to explain why." And he says, "Well, that's just the way I operate. I'm going to be very decisive and you'll get a yes or you'll get a no, but that's the way I operate." The training I got from him was invaluable. I learned how to present my case very quickly and succinctly.*

Like it or not, your word patterns are being judged. In a 2012 study, a Yale University business professor asked participants to rank order CEOs in four scenarios: as a talkative male or female CEO and as a quiet male or female CEO. The talkative male CEO scored the highest. Here's the really disconcerting part: The quiet female CEO ranked second highest. What the study participants were saying is that a talkative woman in a leadership position is viewed negatively. With use of language, less is more, and clarity is key. Make your words pack a punch. You have less leeway here than men do. Men can filibuster in meetings without the kind of reputational damage that women incur. My point is not to speak up less but to speak *efficiently*.

Performance Reviews and Verbal Composure

Composure plays an important role in the performance review, whether you are on the giving or receiving end. I think we can all agree it's not useful to show too much emotion when you're on the receiving end. You shouldn't cry if you're disappointed in your raise and you shouldn't jump up and do a happy dance if your boss praises you. But how much coaching have you gotten on how to *give* a review . . . with composure? It's an area where I've seen many women stumble.

Reviews can be an interesting experience. In general, women are curious about people. We want to know more about them and to hear their stories. This is appropriate in some work situations, such as when you are trying to build trust with someone.

It's not appropriate in reviews.

Giving someone constructive feedback, good or developmental, is what a review is all about. It's not about doing a deep dive into their psyche. It's not helpful to understand the person so well that you uncover any personal baggage behind why he or she is not doing a job well. What matters is being concise and clear about what the job requirements are and showing how the person needs to meet them going forward. Otherwise you spend a lot of unnecessary emotional energy—and words—trying to play shrink.

As a manager, reviews are a place where you can practice limiting your verbiage to what's necessary. You've planned for it, you know it's coming. Role-play the points you want to make. If the person wants to spend the time sharing personal life stories, bring the conversation back around to your purpose. I'm not suggesting you should be robotic or not have empathy for someone. But you owe it to your teammates to give them the most constructive counsel you can during review time. At most workplaces, reviews are done only once a year, so while good managers provide feedback all the time, this is your most important meeting for teaching purposes. If you want social time, ask your colleague to breakfast or lunch. It doesn't belong in a review.

Words to Avoid

Composure doesn't just apply to official business. Be sure to apply it in even your casual work interactions. Avoid describing your stressed-out condition at work. "Oh, I'm so busy! I'm so stressed!" will only make others feel you can't handle your job. Men are allowed to express emotion at work, such as stress or anger, and get away with it. Kind of ironic, right, given women are always called *sooo emotional.* It's just another rule of the game, like it or not.

Also avoid telling your office non-friends things like how hungry you are, some body rash you may be carrying around, or details regarding how your date went last night. These pieces of your personal life or physical state belong only within your work inner circle, which is usually just a couple of people. "I'm starving," "I've contracted this strange disease," or "You can't believe the creep I went out with last night" are all just too much sharing, and for a good gamer observing you, they could indicate vulnerabilities.

Get Training and Practice

Composure isn't a knack, it's a skill—one that can be learned. When I first served on Churchill Downs Incorporated's board, Tom Meeker was CEO. I observed how he spoke in a very precise and orderly way, and later I asked him about it. Turns out he was trained to speak this way during his time as an officer in the Marines. He learned a means of communication called SMEAC, which stands for situation, mission, execution, administration and logistics, and command and signal. In a very few words it communicates a commander's mission and goals, and today it's used at Harvard Business School as a business plan format.

Regal's CEO Amy Miles told me she was precise and concise with language from her Wall Street training. She would go into a meeting with investors and have only thirty minutes to make her point. If you're not succinct, you're out, and you've missed an opportunity to convince a potential investor to buy in.

I trained myself through role-plays and rehearsals. After observing that those men and women who were most effective chose words carefully and with the most punch, I always rehearsed the one or two

points I wanted to leave people with when I had the luxury of knowing a meeting's purpose in advance. However, the reality of life is
spontaneous interaction (better known as having a conversation) so
I just worked to use fewer words to get my thoughts across.

I also learned succinct speaking habits through giving deposi-
tions, which is not something I would wish on anyone. Most business
executives will encounter a lawsuit or two, and about the only thing
they're good for is training in how to keep quiet. Nervous blather
is the downfall of many deposed. Answers that are cropped very
short always work best.

Finally, you learn from experience, so take the opportunity to
step up and speak. When I first began presenting to analysts, I would
accompany bosses Ken Lowe, then CEO of HGTV, and Frank Gardner, then vice president of broadcast operations for E. W. Scripps.
Both were master presenters, and I was about a C. The first time we
were in New York and I got up to speak, I kept hearing feedback
from the mike. Finally Frank, who was sitting nearby, whispered
(more like shrieked): "Move away from the mike! You're popping it!"
I did as instructed and the feedback went away. Live and learn.

How you speak is a combination of presentation style, word
choice, and cadence. Recall Valley girls. They use, like, lots of *likes*
in their language. One *Seinfeld* episode made "close talkers" famous,
those folks who get right into your personal space to convey a point.
There's "upspeak," which is what many Brits do, where the last word
of a sentence is emphasized up, like a question being asked instead
of a statement being made. Then there's my personal favorite, "corporate drone." Don't think I need to explain that one. You've likely
been in that audience far too many times.

There are many classes and programs you can attend to learn
how to speak powerfully and effectively. You will be taped, which is

the best way to learn because it's the naked truth about how you sound.

SELF-CARE

Composure isn't just an emotional state. It has physical underpinnings. To handle the stresses of our too-busy lives, which can lead to loss of composure, we need to take care of ourselves.

If you are not in a state of good physical health, you risk emotionally breaking down. By good state I mean you are eating right, sleeping enough, and getting some exercise, which helps both the body and the brain. So where do you find time to get enough sleep and exercise? When I hear that question, it makes me wonder if perhaps women don't realize how important this is for not only their own well-being but for their kids, husbands, families . . . and companies. If you've flown a commercial airline, you've heard the instructions: In the event of an emergency, the oxygen mask may drop down. Put your own mask on first before assisting others.

The message could not be clearer: You can help others only if you haven't already passed out yourself. This is true whether you're talking about helping small children or a company. Self-care methods help you maintain composure, keep your body strong, and care for others.

I find time in the morning before work to exercise because I'm not an evening exerciser. Exercise of any sort, including walking for a dedicated time, releases mood-boosting endorphins. Since I love my endorphins and they love me right back, I carve out time three or four mornings a week for exercise.

Regarding eating well, I packed a lunch before we built a cafeteria so I could stay away from fast-food row, which was just outside the door. I've always guzzled lots of water, ever since I read somewhere it would keep my skin young. (Hey, action, not motive, is what matters!) Water is nature's elixir; it is so good for you. Make it a habit to keep a bottle with you.

If you're single and think hours at the office are a bigger priority than taking care of yourself, you'll pay the price over time. Good health stretches your peak years for a rich, rewarding career.

Part of good health is knowing how many hours of sleep you need at night, then getting them. You'd be surprised the number of people who don't know how much sleep their bodies need. When you're tired, you lose your sense of humor pretty quickly. You're slower on your feet. It's just plain harder to think and to problem solve.

(New mothers and dads are exempt from that last paragraph.)

If you get the right food, water, exercise, and sleep, you can better manage your energy at work and at home. Some people are born with lots of energy; others are low-energy types. Knowing this about yourself, and getting into good health patterns, will help make the days more productive and enjoyable, and you will be less likely to lose composure and break down in stressful situations.

Know Your Personality Type

Avoiding stress is easier to do if you know whether you're an introvert or extrovert. I am an extrovert, getting surges of energy from other people around me. Introverts, however, need less noise, fewer people, and time for their brains to decompress. You can learn which you are from personality tests and online sites. Once you know, it helps you manage your energy. Both introverts and extroverts are successful CEOs; one's not a better way to be. Besides, you can't change it. What you can do is to adapt to your environments once you have this knowledge in hand.

Patrician McCarthy, author and founder of the Mien Shiang Institute, teaches adapting to your work culture through coming to know how you make decisions. Knowing this is not an easy thing for many women, she argues, because they have been programmed since childhood to make decisions by adapting to others instead of their true selves. She says you can learn how you innately make decisions by how you respond to new and unexpected situations. In her teaching there are five reactions: anger, worry, scattered thoughts, being frozen, or fear. Once you identify which of these is your reaction to unexpected situations, you can train yourself to have counterbalancing reactions.

Lest you think I am into navel gazing by all this self-discovery, I have only one purpose—being composed at work, which maximizes your playing time on the field called business. Poor health habits and poor self-knowledge can lead to emotional breakdowns (errors and fumbles in sports parlance) at work. Reactions to stress are controllable with some good health habits and self-knowledge.

Try Meditation

Meditation is a great way to build and maintain composure. That's something I learned rather late in my career.

I grew up thinking meditation and other practices of silence were done by some weirdos not well grounded on Planet Earth. As an adult, I have done a complete 180. I learned how to meditate at a Centering Prayer retreat in Sewanee, Tennessee. I practice daily, and it's a huge stress reliever. It's remarkable how taking slow, rhythmic breaths can stabilize the mind. It can also train our minds to push away distracting thoughts and to find a peaceful calm. Just as we need exercise, food, rest, and sleep, so too do we need moments of interior silence for the deepest kind of refreshment.

If you watch any baseball, you see the deep breaths that pitchers and hitters take all the time to calm themselves before performing. Another benefit: Learning rhythmic breathing helps you be gentle with yourself and others and lessens your sometimes knee-jerk reactions to people and things. Meditation takes twenty minutes, about the same amount of time it takes to buy a great pair of shoes that you don't need. It takes practice, like all the rules of the game. It took me a couple of years to feel comfortable with meditation and to truly relax this frenetic brain of mine.

I love this meditation story: Buddha was asked what he had gained from meditation. He replied, "Nothing. However, let me tell you what I lost: anger, anxiety, depression, insecurity, and fear." That's a recipe for composure.

Meditation has lots of fans in the C-suite. Padmasree Warrior, chief technology and strategy officer of Cisco Systems, is responsible for leading major market transitions in her company. She helps direct technology and operational innovation across the company and oversees strategic partnerships, mergers, and acquisitions. *Forbes* named her one of the world's 100 most powerful women two years in a row. And she meditates every night to "reboot" her brain and regain her sense of calm. Media mogul Oprah Winfrey is a fan of Transcendental Meditation, as is Executive Management Associates CEO Nancy Slomowitz. In fact, Nancy liked mediation as a workplace booster so much that she rolled it out for employees as an on-site benefit.

If you're not ready for the daily time commitment of meditation, try yoga. It can also be a tremendous benefit to building and maintaining composure. So while you might think of yoga as trying to bend like a pretzel, as I first did, it is a place where one can get a little exercise but also some quiet and spiritual time. It's actually defined as a physical, mental, and spiritual practice. There are beginner classes that put less emphasis on the physical and more on the mental and spiritual. Massage is another great stress reliever. When you relax your body, it softens your mind, opening up more creative thinking.

Alcohol as a Stress Reliever?

I have always had one sales role or another in my career and have attended literally hundreds of cocktail parties and dinners where alcohol was served. At a few of these, sad to say, I drank too much and lost my composure. I should have listened to the advice of my HBO mentor Bill Grumbles, a shrewd Texan, who said this to me early in my career: "Now, Susan, when we go to the cable shows ya gotta wear a helmet on your liver." I was just plain lucky that my episodes with cocktails didn't damage my career.

Risky situations can occur in after-hours work environments of many kinds, including cocktail parties, small dinners, team retreats, or one-on-one time spent with a work colleague. If you're inebriated it's much harder to extract yourself because you have less physical and mental control. That can be a safety issue for you, which it was for me in an instance you will read about later in the book. But as important, it is *not cool* to lose your composure in this way around work colleagues.

Today at cocktail events, there are always options that are nonalcoholic. Stick to those drinks or keep one drink in your hand for the duration. Why risk it? By keeping your head in the game you won't lose composure or say something stupid and have a couple of people walk away muttering, "Wow, did she just *say* that?"

Composure may be a quiet competency, but it's one that can help you no matter what situation you encounter.

YOUR TURN

1. Carry yourself with dignity and calm, signaling to others you're in control, even if you don't always feel it. People can see and know only your actions, not your thoughts or insecurities. Learn how to *act* the role of cool if you need to. However, it's great to show passion for something you believe in and to cheerlead when it's called for.

2. Good health habits and good self-knowledge will help you to manage stress, a frequent cause of loss of composure.

3. If you feel tears coming on, quietly excuse yourself before they appear and make your way to the restroom or outside. Settle yourself, then return.

4. Take a moment to observe the facial expressions you commonly use. Work on a pleasant, not off-putting expression.

5. When speaking or presenting, make every word pack a punch. Your goal is impact and efficiency.

6. You can mentally role-play the one or two points you want to make in advance of scheduled meetings and group presentations to maximize their impact.

7. Reviews should focus on constructive feedback and acknowl-

edgment of good work done, not playing shrink for an employee.

8. There are many excellent before- and after-work stress relievers, including meditation, yoga, and massage.

9. Avoid alcohol or stick to one drink at work events. Getting loose can mean losing your composure.

Chapter 3

Learn to Play Offense

RULE 3: PLAYING OFFENSE

The Game Context: Offense is the action of scoring points. It's the mental and physical state of forward motion in the heat of the contest. It's the condition of possessing the ball or being on the team attempting to score. Offense is the state in which goals are scored, games are won, and glory is achieved.

The Business Setting: Playing offense is being in the front lines and taking actions to improve the business you're in, along with your career. It means asking for what you need to be successful. It may sometimes require *fighting* for things you need to be successful. You may be the stellar behind-the-scenes player who keeps the trains running, but it's the person out in front, making the deal, scoring with new, winning ideas, who gets the attention, the promotion, and the key roles in leadership.

PLAYING VERBAL OFFENSE

In this chapter I discuss how to play offense in asking for what you need to succeed. You can be talking to one person, to a team, or to untold millions at a TED talk. You are using your words to score points, which is everything from new resources to new career opportunities. You can get what you need only by asking for it.

Here's a great example. Amy Miles rose to be CEO of Regal Entertainment. But before that crowning achievement, she was a hardworking senior member of the company's finance team. How did she make it into the top slot? Take a look at this illustration of well-played verbal offense.

The CFO job became vacant. Amy's CEO, Mike Campbell, was very supportive of her getting the job and discussed it with the private equity owners at the time. They recommended she be made interim CFO. Mike came back to her with this idea.

Amy said to him: "I can't do that. I can't be interim CFO. Our investors won't take me or the company seriously. I believe I'm ready for the CFO job. But if I don't get it I'll be here for you to train the new CFO and see if it all works out for me. But I can't take the acting role."

No yelling. No dramatics. But Amy played verbal offense. She made her case respectfully, artfully, arguing how the company would be disadvantaged and, politely but assertively, stating to her boss that she was ready. Shortly thereafter, she was made CFO. Today she runs the company.

Some words, well delivered, can set the stage for success. Nancy Pelosi, representing California in Congress, was on the brink of being the first female Speaker of the House when she stepped up to face a phalanx of microphones at a press conference. She began to talk but reporters in the back called out that they couldn't hear her.

Pelosi, rather than stepping back to let the tech crew handle the glitch, played verbal offense. Pulling herself up to her full five feet, five inches, she powered out to the crowd: "I could use my mother-of-five voice!"

The *New York Times* called her delivery "commanding." Verbal offense is a powerful tool.

I recall a time when I was on the receiving end of verbal offense. As we were situating employees in offices and cubes at HGTV, Robyn Ulrich walked into my office. Robyn was hired to do work in the call center and new media areas. She wanted to understand why it was she hadn't gotten an office. (This business of assigning office space is one of the least favorite things a person in charge has to do.) I had overlooked how Robyn was situated. She argued politely but forcefully that she would have many confidential meetings with prospective partners, and there was training she would need to do that would be noisy to others. She was right. She got an office.

I like to call this kind of verbal offense "artful assertiveness." It's about impact, but as important, it's about finesse. What does being artfully assertive mean? It means communicating direct honesty with a smile. It's backbone without breaking someone's back. It is clearly, respectfully asking for what we need—for ourselves, for the team, or for the company—to succeed.

So let me start with what finesse and artful assertiveness don't look like, starring my departed, beloved aunt Elsie. She loved that I was in business and wanted to make sure I had enough Greek backbone to be successful. So she once told me the story of how she was working as a waitress at an upscale Detroit restaurant called Sinbad's.

World War II had ended; everyone was in a good mood and spending money. Her tips were great. There was a cook there named George, and all the waitresses were afraid of him, except Aunt Elsie. One night someone bumped her arm and she dropped her tray of six full dinners. She had to go back to the kitchen to tell George to remake all the dinners, and she knew it wouldn't be pleasant. As she tells it, she walked in and said, "George, I dropped my tray and you can either remake the food or go fuck yourself!"

Good ole George made those dinners.

This approach may have worked for Aunt Elsie, but that's not the kind of assertiveness I'm recommending. Shouting, confronting, even dropping the F-bomb will get you attention, but as strategy, it lacks finesse. You need diplomacy to win in the workplace.

But you also need resources to win—resources that will allow you to do your job better, like more capital or people, and enhancements to your work conditions, such as a raise or promotion. You need to take the floor and be heard in any number of ways. *If you don't ask, you don't get.*

Being a woman, however, *how* you ask for things matters. There are all kinds of B-words (*bitch, ballbuster, bossy*) that might be used to describe you if you don't ask with the right finesse. Sheryl Sandberg teamed up with Girl Scouts of the USA to launch a public service campaign around the word *bossy*, pointing out its pejorative connotations for girls today and how we could work to change that. The Ban Bossy campaign has attracted celebrity support, including Beyoncé and Jane Lynch.

Finding the right balance in asking for things isn't easy. The flip side of coming on too strong is that you can also be painfully polite when it comes to asking. This can trip you up too. When you are painfully polite, there is no power behind the ask. Picture a woman in a performance review saying, "I really think I've done a good job and I've tried really, really hard and if it's not too much of a burden, do you think there's room for me in a more senior role?" Or picture another scenario: "You've shared in my reviews praise for my work. Might we now talk about what career advancement looks like for me in this company?" It's easy for anyone hearing that painfully polite delivery to say no because they think you won't challenge them. When you are painfully polite, you telegraph your expectation that the answer will be no.

Never forget that your competition inside the company is asking for things too, and company resources are finite. You need to hold your ground when you're asking. You need a strong and certain voice. Joan Cronan, former athletic director at the University of Tennessee, called it the right level of volume to be heard.

WOMEN, MEDIA, AND THE NEED FOR ARTFUL OFFENSE

Gender stereotyping remains pervasive in our culture, even as women make advances on every front. In January 2014, *Time* published an issue with an image of Hillary Clinton's pant leg squashing a tiny man hanging from her heel. There was a vocal, online outcry to such imagery because it once again paints a negative portrayal of women leaders as emasculating men. I've made a career in media, and some of my brothers and sisters in the business are purveyors of negative, stereotypical images of women leaders. In some cases, they either present these outdated portraits, or they leave women out where they should be represented.

As we were getting HGTV off the ground, there was only one

other cable network that was specifically geared to women, and that was Lifetime. When we pitched HGTV, one prospective client asked, "Is that a chick channel?" Today there must be twenty different ESPN channels, and a boatload of other cable networks appealing to men. The latest is the World Fishing Network, "the only TV channel dedicated to fishing." Amid all of this, there are still relatively few women's networks.

Here's another case in point from the business of motion pictures. Since 1998 a San Diego State professor has been researching the presence of women on the business side of motion pictures as well as percentage of time on the screen. The 2013 research revealed that the percentage of women behind the camera has actually decreased since 1998 when examining the 250 top-grossing films of 2013. The numbers were in single digits or in the teens, depending on the job. On the screen, women had 30 percent of speaking parts when looking at the top 100 films. Both off the screen and on the screen, women lag men dramatically.

Amy Miles shares this from a time when she served on a panel with actress and producer Geena Davis:

> *Geena did this study, which showed that, in crowd scenes, 17 percent of the people are female. Just 17 percent! I'm sorry, but 17 percent of the world is not female. There's a theory in Hollywood that it's easier to convince a female to go to an action-oriented male-lead movie than it is to convince a man to go a female-lead movie. My sons go to* Hunger Games *for Jennifer Lawrence, pure and simple. These practices are just bad business.*

The absence of women is leaving money on the table everywhere, and playing artful offense is one key solution.

Some Great Examples

Sue Falsone is the first female head trainer of a major sports team, the Los Angeles Dodgers. The physical aspect of sports training is only a part of her job. The rest is communication. She has to ask the players to cooperate with her so they can stay in good health to play well. She has to ask them to work with her when they're disabled by injuries, which is even harder. Players praise her ability to balance being pushy and sensitive at the same time. Sue developed a communications style that is both assertive and artful—she can get those testosterone-happy athletes to see things her way without the bravado and bluster associated with sports. It's an assertiveness born of strategy.

Philip Orbanes is a game designer and author, and he studies gamers, especially Monopoly players. He has been a chief judge at the U.S. and World Monopoly championships. Anyone who has played Monopoly knows you're always asking to trade properties and to make good deals so you can win. Philip wrote a book about this board game and its broader implications. In it, he tells the story of the 2009 championship in which a young Norwegian player won not only by being inventive but by asking competitors for trades and deals in a way that was respectful and pleasant. He diverged quite obviously from his noisy and aggressive competitors. He won, and others didn't seem to mind losing to him. His game strategy is a good example of artful assertiveness. He got his way not by shouting and pounding his chest but by engaging.

Here's one artfully assertive example from my own history. In the early days of frantically preparing HGTV to be launched, the founding team had a meeting to agree upon the launch date. I was one of the few in the room with a cable industry background and was hired to use that expertise. When we had finally agreed on a launch date I said (with a smile), "I'm so glad we got that important thing done, so we can begin plans for our next cable network."

Next cable network? Had I lost my mind? We'd barely scrambled through a launch decision for HGTV and I was suggesting the *next* network?

I had five sets of eyes on me that were flashing everything from disbelief to anger. One of the guys looked like he wanted to execute a low tackle and take me out. Another colleague looked as if his head were going to blow off. They could not believe that right then, at that moment, I was bringing this up. But I kept at it, explaining how the industry was morphing to digital platforms and we needed to land some of that real estate once HGTV had its footing. The nascent network concept, the seed of which was planted that day, came to be called the DIY Network. Today it's a nice, profitable business for SNI.

What I did in that room was make a clear offensive move as preparation to score our next big win. I could see the potential in the next network. It's like a moment in sports when a player sees the whole field, and her teammates fall into line around her. That's what happened that day. I didn't ramrod my point; I pushed through their dismay with the facts about our distributors and how they had begun to transition to digital platforms. I painted a picture rich with promise for our fledgling company. The seed I planted that day took root a few years later. My artful assertiveness opened the door.

When I asked one of my colleagues about this meeting much later he would say I sounded pretty darn sure this was how we should go. I sounded full of conviction. I can tell you I wasn't feeling that way. I thought things like, I know this going to be ugly. I'll get hard looks and cold words. They'll think I'm a board-certified lunatic.

This is how I felt, but this wasn't what my words said. You will read this nugget many times in the book. Gamesmanship sometimes has nothing to do with how you feel on the inside. Offense can require aggressive moves that may not flow naturally out of you, but with enough repetitions you'll get comfortable with practicing this important rule.

VERBAL OFFENSE IN COMPENSATION

Data continue to confirm that women are still behind men in compensation for the same jobs. If you're willing to live with that, that's your business. But I wasn't. As my job was morphing in the early 1990s into faux lawyer from salesperson, I knew there should be more compensation. I was doing harder, more complex work. So I called a headhunter friend, Ann Carlsen, founder of Carlsen Resources, and asked her to share what the going rates were for this job. The averages would take into account the guys doing this job too, and the majority of those running this area were men. Ann shared this with me so I was armed with data for comp discussions, and I successfully received the comp I was due. It's hard to argue with data, says Amy Miles of Regal. She continues:

> *When you're coming from behind, you're going to have to do more to bridge that gap. Maybe you're fighting an expectation gap that a male isn't, and you're fighting a salary gap. It doesn't work to go in and say, "You should pay me more because I think I'm worth more." You should have the research and say, "Here are the data I found, and I expect to be compensated like my peers."*

VERBAL OFFENSE IN PROMOTIONS

You should ask for promotions. Are you about ready? I say "about" because none of us is perfectly ready to take our next step up, when you think about it. How can we capably do that next job with bigger responsibility when we've never done it before? When you are *about* ready, you should begin having discussions with your supervisor, laying out what you would like to do next. Think broadly. Look around your organization at the various openings one rung up that could be suitable for your skills and background. I wouldn't recommend doing this in your first twelve or eighteen months because you need to prove yourself to those around you first. But if after about two years you can see your next role, go for it. Do mental role-plays so you can project what your supervisor may say, determine how he or she may challenge you, and be prepared to return the volleys.

You should also *accept* promotions, when offered. Women can be shy and insecure about accepting a newer, bigger job because we don't feel we're ready. Ask yourself, How would a man respond to this job offer? Would he waffle? Would he say he's not sure he's ready? Most men would not.

Joan Cronan says, "I've hired men who I felt like were in the car coming before I offered them the job. And women will say, Call me back in two weeks." She spoke of a young woman who was very talented and wanted to be an athletic director like Joan. She had two questions for Joan: "'Do I have to give speeches?' And I told her yes, [she] had to be willing to be in the public. And she said, two, 'Do I have to leave Jefferson City?' And I said yes. She is now a wonderful accountant in Jefferson City, Tennessee."

You have to take care of yourself in the workplace because no one else will. You might get a mentor or two along the way, but ultimately the management of your career falls squarely on your own two shoulders. You need to play verbal offense, asking for and accepting opportunities, raises, and promotions if you want to advance.

Amy Miles says:

My dad always said, "When you leave this house, no one cares." And in a way he was right. We may have great mentors and will find people at work to help us along, but you still have to take responsibility for your own career. My spouse isn't going to take care of this for me; my parents aren't going to take care of this for me. Everything about my career is up to me.

This is taking personal responsibility. The great news is it's up to you to find all the opportunities to advance. The bad news—if you're not playing offense—is that it will be an uphill battle to find the opportunities to advance.

If you can't get a good handle on what it takes to be artfully assertive, practice. Think about situations that will allow you to "make an ask" and give it a shot. Start with something that could help your company so it doesn't look self-serving, like I did with DIY. Make the pitch to your supervisor. Then make a pitch for some resources that could help your team to do better work, perhaps a new piece of technology or some needed research. Be sure you have your ducks in a row with logic and, if possible, data to support your request.

IT'S OK TO BE A LITTLE BOSSY

It's better to be bossy than to be painfully shy, at least it is with career advancement. There's that old adage about it being better to ask for forgiveness than for permission. I'm guessing this was invented by a man, but it's great advice for us. Toward the end of my time with Amy Miles, she told me a story about her young niece and nephew, Holland and Ben. She would watch Ben tell Holland that they were going to play Batman, whom he would be, and Holland was to be Robin.

Later Holland would say, "OK, now we're going to play I'm the librarian and you're the student," and the adults watching would tell her she was being too bossy. She needed to stop that. After observing this, Amy pulled Holland aside and said it's OK to be a little bossy. That's a good thing.

I'm hopeful that young girls will not need lessons in artful assertiveness. Once, when I spoke to a group of women leaders, there was a woman in the audience with her nine-year-old daughter. I shared a childhood story of a neighborhood beauty pageant and my competitive streak. The night before the voting I made this gorgeous sash that spelled out, with my mom's help, C-O-N-T-E-S-T-A-N-T and strutted around the block the next day with it on, like I'd already won. (I also bribed the kid judges with candy, but that's another story.) Clearly I was trying to stack the deck for a win.

After the speech the little girl came up to me and she said, "Why did your sash say *contestant*? Why didn't it say *winner*?" If it weren't against child labor laws, I would have hired her on the spot.

Here's an adult version of what it means to be artfully assertive.

This is a popular joke, but it illustrates my point and should make you smile, at least if you're female.

A woman and her CEO husband were taking a drive in the country one day, and her husband stopped for gas. He saw his wife get out of the car and walk over to the gas station attendant. After they chatted she got back in the car, and she told her husband she had known that man when they were teens. In fact, they had dated.

Her husband looked at her after a moment and said, "I bet I know what you're thinking. You're thinking you're glad you married me, a high-powered CEO, rather than him, some gas station attendant." "No," she said without pause. "I was thinking if I'd married him he'd be a high-powered CEO and you'd be a gas station attendant."

Now would you call that bossy, or artfully assertive?

YOUR TURN

1. Because you are more likely to get labeled with one of those B-words if you come on too strong, ask for resources with artful assertiveness. Ask clearly, directly, and respectfully. Avoid bulldozing your way through requests, which can be off-putting.
2. When asking for resources, include rationale that will benefit the company.
3. When asking for a raise, have data on comparable positions within your industry. Any industry headhunter can supply such data.
4. Realize no one on the planet is fully prepared to take a job

with increased responsibility. If one is offered, take it! We sometimes don't get second chances.

5. Be willing to ask for promotions if you are 80 percent ready. Practice mental role-plays for the discussion you will have with your supervisor, and keep your discussion points short and pithy, especially if presenting to a man. As these discussions gain traction, see item 3. Don't forget—if you don't ask, you will definitely not get. You set yourself up to never win in your career. But if you play some offense, you put yourself squarely on the playing field.

Chapter 4

Master the Strategies of Brinksmanship

RULE 4: BRINKSMANSHIP STRATEGIES

The Game Context: Brinksmanship is the strategy in which we gain an advantage without clearly stating our goals. In poker, it's the art of reading the tell. In Monopoly, it's the insight that tells you when to walk away from a property trade. Gut instincts and subtle cues play a big part.

The Business Setting: Brinksmanship is the skill of artful negotiations, with a little bit of theater thrown in. In politics, brinksmanship has a slightly different meaning. It's more literal: all about taking the situation to the brink. In this book, I use it to describe a high-level negotiating mind-set. It's about using strategies to appraise your position and making decisions to get an advantage. Whether it's a contract negotiation or an acquisition, through brinksmanship you can turn a deal your way in a quick and subtle fashion. Victories go to those who can leverage their understanding of people and the marketplace to make winning moves. Practicing brinksmanship makes you a champion gamer.

MY INTRODUCTION TO BUSINESS BRINKSMANSHIP

In the early days of building HGTV, I asked my CEO, Ken Lowe, to accompany me on a sales call. It's often a good tactic to bring the big brass on early calls, signaling your respect for the opponent. We traveled to Denver, home of the biggest and baddest prospect during that time, called Tele-Communications Inc. (TCI). They played ridiculous mind and leverage games in doing deals, and it was an ugly, bloody process to get business done. However, TCI had the most subscribers in the cable industry, and we needed access to their systems to get adequate distribution for HGTV.

When we arrived, we were ushered into a waiting room, where we proceeded to do just that—wait, for two hours. Upon inquiring, we learned our client had made a dental appointment he'd forgotten to tell his assistant—or us—about. I figured then that this would end (if it ever began) with some serious brinksmanship at play. We were finally brought into the conference room and the client walked in. I looked at his teeth. No drooling, no pearly whites. Likely no dental appointment.

We quickly got down to business. He stated his company's position, which was ridiculous. Not a big surprise, given that with every passing year their reputation as bullies gained steam in the industry. Even given that, I was surprised at how intransigent he was being. His edicts were nonstarters. I knew there was only one way to play this. After about fifteen minutes, I stood and declared the meeting over. Always a cool customer, Ken stood and we walked away. By the look on my potential client's face, I could tell he saw I'd called an audible.

As Ken and I climbed into the rental car he asked, "Susan, why did that meeting go so badly?" Ken was accustomed to civilized people, which wasn't exactly the norm in cable TV. When the industry was growing up in the 1970s and 1980s, there was fraternity and shared common interests; later it was all about one-sided wins.

"It hadn't gone badly," I told Ken. "Actually we won that round. They wanted us to beg. We needed to tilt the power in our favor. That was just round one." TCI called a few weeks later. It took two long years to close that deal, but we got it done, and it brought us the needed national distribution footprint, plus tens of millions of dollars to HGTV.

It is just this kind of deal making in which you can perfect the art of business brinksmanship. These situations may seem worrisome when you're in them, but in fact, they are good, healthy challenges that will test and grow your mental agility. This is the work that will help you to see that business is one big game. Doing deals provides a thrilling adrenaline rush. After every session you can evaluate what was accomplished and whether that time spent was a win or a loss. And as you enter into such deals and evaluate your own performance, you'll begin to see the impact of brinksmanship strategies. If it was a team negotiation, evaluate the session together, regroup, then go back in for the next round.

Brinksmanship is a strategic process of outsmarting your opponent to get the win. Ideally you want to engage in win–win outcomes for both sides, but sometimes the person across the table wants to sweep up all the chips. This was the environment in the cable TV industry and perhaps where you work as well. Try for the win–win, but if that's not happening, you'll need brinksmanship strategies to secure the best possible deal.

The strategies involved in brinksmanship most closely pattern thinking games, like chess, checkers, and cards. Chess is especially relevant here because it might be the most cerebral, yet strategic, game around. Case in point are the winning strategies of women's world chess champion, Hou Yifan of China. As of this writing, she is close to being named to the top 100 of all chess champions, men and women. Only one other woman has ever attained such stature. At a recent tournament, she played former women's world champion Antoaneta Stefanova of Bulgaria. Antoaneta lost to Hou because her strategy was to postpone castling to get to Hou's pawn, which allowed Hou to use some brinksmanship to attack and win.

In business, brinksmanship comes into play with a wide range of jobs. Most line jobs will require deal making, whether you're in sales or product development or are head of a division or department. You will find yourself negotiating with clients and vendors for the best deals you can bring back to your company. You engage in a process of role-plays and rehearsals and gather the opponent's facts and figures. Then, like a soccer player who visualizes where she wants the ball to go before she kicks it, you visualize where you want to end up. You begin at the end, determining what the expected outcome should be through management's guidance or the financial parameters already laid out for you, like an internal rate of return (IRR). It's best to work with a *range* of acceptable outcomes, from the least desirable (or "bottom") to the most desirable, so you can be more creative and agile while you are closing in on the win. Whatever your most desirable outcome is, start above it when you are engaging your opponent.

PERSONAL BRINKSMANSHIP

Brinksmanship can get quite personal, which is something you should always avoid. I once read a comment that fencing is like chess with the risk of puncture wounds. Well, negotiating can be a lot like fencing. You need to avoid puncture wounds on either side of the table. If you walk into the room and your opponent says, "Your mama's ugly!," this could be a bad sign. While it's OK for linebackers to trash talk on the field, it's never OK to get personal in a negotiation. People have long memories, and it will come back to haunt you. Having said that, men often like to try to bully as a tactic in deal making. This is one of their versions of theater. They may rant and rave, but it's not personal. These are tactics to disarm you. I learned this through the repetitions I got at the negotiating table, working mostly with men. Over time you get better discerning the drama meant to disarm you. It's like watching a pro basketball game in which a player drops to the ground hoping for a foul call, flopping and flailing, and fooling no one. With some experience, you can spot it.

In the 2012 film *Arbitrage*, Richard Gere plays a character named Robert Miller. There's a great scene where he and his opponent are screaming at each other and carrying on during a negotiation. Then Robert Miller threatens to publicly embarrass his opponent. These are all seemingly personal, below-the-belt tactics. A few moments later they're both smiling, having found middle ground and acknowledging they each made a good deal. No hard feelings. It's not personal, it's business.

In my experience a lot of men (more so than women) carry on in negotiations like they are on personal attack, but it's just a tactic. Some guys playing contact sports have used their bodies as human steamrollers growing up. They see deal making as just another aggressive contact sport. They're trying to bulldoze their way to an outcome that benefits only them. Again, this is a version of theater. Respond in kind with your own style of brinksmanship. Hold your ground and feign indifference. It puts the power in your hands.

My colleague Ruth Tatom would scream, "Everybody out of the pool!" when our clients were throwing tantrums and basically acting like children. That got their attention. If this behavior gets under your skin, end the session, and tell your client you expect to be treated respectfully or there won't be any future engagements. It's important on both sides of the table to have a healthy respect for the opponent, and if one side truly does not, both sides risk a poor outcome. The bully puts the other party on the defensive, which shuts off creative problem solving.

Brinksmanship is a combination of theater, observational skills, and mental agility. Although the strategy involves many moves, I will highlight four of them. They are often used to get back the advantage, as deal making progresses. Anyone who has sat at the negotiating table knows that the advantages ebb and flow, and we look for ways to regain them.

Breaking It Down

Here are some key moves to employ in the process of business brinksmanship, which come from card games:

- The Walk Away
- The Bluff
- Sizing Up the Room
- The Tell

I'll examine each one, how it works, when to use it, and how you can practice it.

The Walk Away

Ronee Hagen, former CEO of Polymer Group, tells this story:

> I was recruited to a position and the company made me an offer that was below what I thought I was worth. I told them they had a wonderful company, but I would not be interested in the salary range they offered. I then offered to give them some less experienced candidates who might be interested in that pay level. In less than two hours they came back with a much richer offer. The biggest negotiating leverage you ever have is to be able to walk away.

That's an excellent example of this brinksmanship tactic in action. The reality of executing the walk away is hard for a lot of us, so let's talk about that.

The key to the successful walk away is knowledge and preparation. You must know what your bottom is in any deal, which is your least acceptable outcome. You can live with it, but you don't love it. If your opponent has so much leverage due to their market position that your bottom will still be too high for them, it's time to walk away. That is pretty evident early on, like being dealt a bad poker hand when your opponent is holding all the cards. Some deals just can't get done and you have to fold.

In Ronee's case, she knew her bottom. She had enough knowledge to know her own worth in the marketplace, and that gave her the confidence to set her bottom and hold it. It was that knowledge that allowed her to execute the walk away with confidence—and results.

The walk away may be most familiar to us in a compensation

negotiation, but that's not the only way you can use it. As you read
in the chapter's opening story, sometimes you can use the walk away
to send a signal the meeting has been unproductive, and you're end-
ing it. You retain the leverage because you walked, sort of like getting
in the last word.

The Bluff

The bluff is a little sleight of hand that can come in handy in business. Back in my SNI days we used to employ the puffer fish approach, which was to puff up bigger than we really were. Puffer fish
are relatively small and slow and are common in the tropical regions
of South America, Central Africa, and Southeast Asia. When a puffer
is pursued by a predator, it will fill its extremely elastic stomach with
water until it is much larger, rounder, and harder to eat. Its spines
will stick out like spears, and its roundness will offer few easy chomp-
ing points. Many a hungry predator has observed this big, puffy,
pointy-looking thing and decided, "Never mind."

At HGTV we would appear to the industry that we had vast
resources we were putting against R&D initiatives, for example,
when in truth our budgets were very limited, and smaller than our
competition's. We needed to appear as well resourced even though
we were a small, independent startup, with an untested track record.
We blasted to the industry some consistent messaging around R&D,
and the few of us doing the work got ourselves on panels wherever
possible to speak about our efforts.

Back then there were a lot of parties interested in acquiring cable
networks too, and because we had a small, independent parent company, we needed to puff up so the outside world wouldn't think
we were vulnerable to being scooped up, or eaten. Our puffer fish
communication strategies allowed us to compete step by step, and

to stay in the game while we drove toward profitability. The win was moving the business from the red into the black.

Most engaged in business will agree that bluffing is a powerful skill. Done well it sends messages that keep your competition guessing. Talk to any great business leader, and he or she will surely have a bluff story.

Another bluff strategy is to call someone else's bluff, which means knowing someone's trying to fool you and to not fall for it.

Carly Fiorina was president and CEO of Hewlett-Packard, a top Fortune 500 company, from 1999 until 2005. In her book, *Tough Choices*, she describes something that occurred early in her career that tested her willingness to play tough. She had joined AT&T's Government Communications as a sales rep. One of her new clients was the Bureau of Indian Affairs (BIA). A sales colleague who had worked with BIA and had built a legendary relationship with them— and didn't like sharing—told Carly that while representatives of the BIA were coming to town to meet the next day, she would be uncomfortable where they held the meeting. The BIA reps apparently loved having meetings in a DC restaurant called the Board Room, which was actually a strip club. Carly slept on it, reconciling she had been given a tough challenge but she still had a job to do. She told her colleague the next day she would be there, and she went. She called his bluff and stayed in the game. Her colleague couldn't believe it.

Something similar happened to me early in my career. As I was helping to build the HBO business, I called on a new client in a Detroit suburb and asked him to lunch. He said he knew of a place nearby and directed me as I drove. I was born and raised in Detroit but was not familiar with this section of the metro area. Once we arrived, I saw a nondescript building, and the hairs on the back of my neck began to prickle, but there were other cars in the lot so I thought, What's the harm? Plus I was driving and could depart if I needed to. We walked into a place so dark it took a moment for my eyes to adjust, and he rushed me to a table. Once seated, I realized we were in a strip club. He had this triumphant smile on his face that said, I got her here, now what's she going to do? I asked him what point he was trying to make. He said something like, "Well, the food's just great here!" I waited, stared at him, and finally asked for the lunch menu. His bluff was a power challenge, and he lost. As we drove away I properly chastised him for the test he put me through. Shortly thereafter I was promoted to run the region and I put a man on the account. There's brinksmanship, but more importantly, there's safety. Could another woman have handled it as I did? Sure. But as far as I was concerned, there was no reason to put another woman through a test with this moron.

Calling one's bluff is a move showing you're as competitive as your opponent, and you are willing to play as mentally tough as anyone in the business. You see the bluff used a lot in poker, and other games of all kinds involving betting and risk. National Public Radio, for example, has a weekly "Bluff the Listener" segment on the popular *Wait, Wait . . . Don't Tell Me* program. It's also big in business dealings because you are often being tested for your mettle. Hang in there. Don't get sacked. Show 'em you've got the fight in you to win.

Nancy Peterson, a Nashville friend and executive, recalled the time her husband sadly and suddenly passed away in 1979. They owned a precision cutting tool manufacturing company that did business for the metalworking industry, and their clients were all men. She knew many of them, but her husband was the face of the company. Despite her sadness, she decided she would carry on and stepped in as president and CEO, but she worried her clients wouldn't take kindly to a woman in that role.

All their customers were out of state, so she kept her husband's passing quiet and personal for many months, traveling around the country visiting and updating clients on her company's progress. On one call she was asked, "Where is John? I haven't seen him for a while." She shared that he had passed away six months before, and she was now in charge. He offered condolences, then looked at her and remarked, somewhat incredulous: "We haven't noticed any difference," and Nancy replied, "Why should you?"

Here's a bluff story that would never, ever happen in today's business world, but it's reflective of how onerous it can be for women to succeed.

A New York friend who was building her IT consulting business in the 1980s faced a dilemma. She knew she had to get into Federal Express and to get their business. But the gatekeepers were all men (and Southern men at that), and they wouldn't return her calls. She came up with a brainstorm: She would hire a good-looking, good-golfing male actor who would play the part of CEO. The two of them would make the call together. She hired him and trained him for weeks on the business. They secured the meeting. He played CEO, and she played his assistant. They had a code that if FedEx asked a question he couldn't answer, he would cough and she would pipe up, "He's got a bronchial condition but I can answer that." And so the meeting went.

After the pitch, the FedEx guys asked him to golf, and then dinner. Now she was worried. What if he couldn't answer a question? What if he got drunk? She paced the halls of the motel like the parent of a teenager waiting for him to get home. Finally the elevator pinged, and he stepped out. "Well?? How did it go?" she asked nervously. "I thunk it wen wul . . . ," he slurred drunkenly.

"NO!" she screamed. But he broke into a smile. He was just teasing. He had successfully played the role, and they would sign the contract the next day. She staged an outrageous bluff, and it worked.

Sizing Up the Room

The brinksmanship skill of sizing up the room is hugely important and often overlooked. Most women are well suited to it because they're observant, and good listeners—which are two skills critical to trying it. Sizing up a room has you assessing your situation, your opponents, your options, and using what you see to gain an advantage. Unlike the walk away and the bluff, this is a tactic that can't be ginned up ahead of time. You need to be quick and observant.

When I joined the board of Churchill Downs Inc., home to the Kentucky Derby, I walked into the first board meeting and noticed that we were all assigned seats, as indicated by place cards. Since this was my first experience as board member with a for-profit, publicly traded company, I assumed it was customary practice. (I would later learn that's not the case.) After I had attended a few board meetings, I noted that while my assigned seat moved around a bit, it was never close to the CEO, whose place at the table never changed. There were also two board members who flanked him, and their position never changed. Those three held most of the power in the room. You couldn't know that from just meeting the players. You had to be in the room, sizing it up for information you could use.

It's important to discern who holds the power when you enter a room. I walked into one negotiation with two people present, and as we commenced reviewing the contract drafts, one of them was turning the pages of the document for the other. My first thought was how sad that was for the poor page turner, but it helped me because it was pretty obvious who held the power. It's not always obvious in the beginning, but soon into a session someone will dominate the discussion and he or she likely hold the power.

However, there are exceptions. Recall that we businesspeople are *line*; our lawyers are *staff.* The line folks will hold the power—even if their lawyers talk incessantly. And lawyers do like to talk. In any event, it's important to size up the room so you can determine whose points you need to pay attention to. Sometimes there are several people across the table, and the balls are being lobbed in from all directions. Always attend to the line executives first.

Sizing up the room also means literally looking around the room, beyond the people to the physical space and the clues it can give you. Once on a sales call with Ken, we went down to Tampa to pitch a client who had a large, regional footprint that would be great real estate for HGTV. I had my PowerPoint presentation ready and my blue business suit pressed and starched, buttons gleaming. I walked in planning to bowl this man over with my dazzling sales presentation.

Just as I was opening up my laptop, Ken commented on the décor of the client's office. It was quite literally a shrine to Elvis Presley. There were photographs from his concerts, framed tickets, collectible posters and memorabilia. Everything but a portrait of the King on black velvet.

Once Ken noted the Elvis theme, those two took off on Elvisisms, and I never even got the computer powered up. Ken closed that deal with a promise to send the client a shipment of Memphis ribs. The moral of the story: Always pay attention to the room you find yourself in. It will tell you what you need to know to compete and win in that arena.

The Tell

If you're a parent, you know that some of your kids fib easily and smoothly. Others have a tell. They look away, they fidget, they tug at their hair or clothing. Everything but hold up a sign saying, "Yes, I broke the lamp in the living room."

These cues extend into adulthood. If you watch closely, you can see that many smart, sophisticated businesspeople have a tell—a physical manifestation that lets you know how they really feel.

Professional poker players will say that winning is not all about odds and probabilities. If you're playing at the top of your game, it's about reading others, watching their physical mannerisms, which tell if they have good cards or not. The tell is body language that conveys something about your opponent. When Oprah Winfrey interviewed disgraced cyclist Lance Armstrong after he was banned from the sport for doping, a body language expert reviewed Armstrong's performance and said he betrayed his fear by looking away from Oprah rather than looking her in the eye, and he kept taking deep breaths and swallowing hard, signs of nervousness and anxiety. He was also wringing his hands, a sign of someone under pressure.

The best way to stay away from your own tells is this: How much you want something is precisely how much you should act like you *don't*. The old adage that says Never let 'em see you sweat applies here. We are expressive beings as women, so playing in this zone of neutrality, or indifference, doesn't come naturally. But if you can step back for a moment and think about tells as a strategy, you'll see that that neutral zone cedes no benefit to your opponent. He can't play on any chinks in your armor to get the win, because you're not conveying anything useful. If, however, your opponent recognizes that you want something badly, that becomes a vulnerability he can exploit as you two work toward an outcome.

Your opponent's tells are always helpful to discern, and some-times they're a pretty easy read. If you walk into a negotiating session and your customer is leaning back in his chair with his feet up on his desk, he's telling you he has the power. He's playing quarterback. Alpha dog. Don't let it throw you. Politely press on. He may try to antagonize you. Don't get baited. Sometimes that Y chromosome can take up the whole room if you let it.

Talking too much can be a tell of nervousness. There is a certain rhythm to a negotiation and moving into the rhythm is important. Both men and women can have a hard time with the silence that should come after your position, or your customer's, is put forward. I had trouble with this too, and learned to count to twenty while I kept eye contact and a smile on my face. No chattering; less is more when doing deals. If you are offering a position, state it and wait. If you are receiving one, it's usually best to listen fully, wait, count to twenty while maintaining eye contact, then respond. Of course if the other person's position is ludicrous or insulting, doing something with theatrical flair like a walk away might be appropriate.

Perhaps the strangest example of the tell that I experienced was with a good guy in the business, whom I was just getting to know. We had some deal work before us. When I first walked into his of-fice, he stood and I realized he was quite short for a man, perhaps five-foot-four. I always wore heels in negotiations to give my puny, five-foot-two frame some stature. We moved into his conference room together and as soon as I sat he seemed to relax, although he did a lot of the negotiating standing and walking around. I'd ask: "Why don't you sit down?" and he'd respond: "I'd rather stand." After a couple of sessions of this, I noticed that his overall demeanor toward me was far more accommodating when he was able to look down at me. The next session, I wore flats, testing a theory I had about the whole dynamic. Sure enough, when I walked into his office to greet him, he stood, clearly comfortable, and we had the most productive session for my company in our short history together. He sat the whole time negotiating, and we comfortably exchanged volleys. He signaled to me, over and over, that he would be more comfortable doing business if he could dominate the room. Well, I'm a businessperson, not a psychologist, but it sure seemed his game was called Power Play, while mine was called Make Money. I saw the need to neutralize the impediments to getting a deal that we could be happy with. I read the tell and I proceeded with the knowledge it gave me. The next couple of times we met I wore flats and we both scored a nice win.

There can be a lot of theater in negotiations that really adds some color and spice to the game.

MOVIES AND TV: GREAT MOMENTS IN BRINKSMANSHIP

You can practice many of the gamesmanship skills I discuss in this book through role-playing and other rehearsals. But when it comes to brinksmanship, you can start the process by firing up the DVD player or Apple TV box. Many of the brinksmanship skills I'm suggesting for business success are often tapped by TV and screen-writers to achieve dramatic effect. Here are a few of my favorites:

The Walk Away: Cinema is full of heroes who hold fast to their principles and know their bottom. In *Wall Street*, Bud Fox walks away from the world run by Gordon Gekko, even though it will cost him his freedom.

The Bluff: No film does this better than *The Sting*. Henry

Gondorff (Paul Newman) and Johnny Hooker (Robert Redford) weave a complex Prohibition-era scam, and everyone is bluffing everyone throughout the picture. At a dramatic turn in the storyline, Henry even delivers advice to his young protégé on the art of bluffing and why you can't bluff your friends.

A TV series with bluffs and brinksmanship is Netflix's *House of Cards*. The show's anti-hero, Frank Underwood, spends most of season two bluffing his nemesis, Raymond Tusk. In one scene they confront each other and Frank tells Raymond, "The sign of a good bluffer is when he makes you believe he's not."

Sizing Up the Room: In the classic film *Casablanca*, protagonist Rick Blaine does a wonderful job sizing up the room early in the film. Fans of the movie may remember a scene in Rick's Café Américain in which he sits down and has a drink with the visiting Vichy dignitaries. His character is carefully assessing the threat the visitors pose, the possibilities he may have in countering them, and the larger challenges that loom in the backdrop of his personal drama. It's the setup for Rick's final act of heroism on the tarmac with his beloved Ilsa.

The Tell: *The Usual Suspects* has tells throughout the film, along with one great bluff. Following a truck hijack in New York, five con men are arrested. None of them is guilty, and they plan a revenge operation against the police. The operation goes well, but then the influence of a legendary mastermind criminal called Keyser Söze comes into play. It becomes clear that each of the con men has wronged Söze at some point and it is now payback time. The payback job leaves twenty-seven men dead in a boat explosion, and a question arises: Who actually is Keyser Söze? Can you spot the tells he leaves throughout the story? In the final minutes of the film, watch the actor's eyes shift, and see how the cop finally figures it all out.

Shonda Rhimes, creator of *Grey's Anatomy*, weaves a show around tells in her latest ABC series *Scandal*. The lead protagonist, Olivia Pope, is a behind-the-scenes Washington, DC, fixer. She and her team decide to take on new clients by screening them for their various tells.

WHY DO MANY OF US LACK BRINKSMANSHIP SKILLS?

Think back to the playground and the rules you played by as a child. What did girls and boys value? And how did those rules differ?

In many cases, we may remember that we were often concerned with fair play. No cheating. No breaking the rules. Games were played aboveboard, and girls valued friends who lived by this creed.

Many boys, on the other hand, received a more win-at-all-costs message. This wasn't perceived to be immoral or unethical, it was how you played the game. Boys were coached to steal bases, steal the ball, fake left, break right. Can you think of a game played predominantly by girls in which the Walk Away, the Bluff, Sizing Up the Room, or the Tell played a role? The closest I can come is hide-and-seek. And for me, at least, I was always excited when I was found and laughed and hugged my seeker.

As we grew up, our games followed these same patterns. Boys grew into men who went into business and continued to practice brinksmanship. Girls grew into women who formed their own social circles that rarely encouraged anything but open, clear interactions. Today girls play many team sports, and some of them, through college years. With this new generation, gender behavioral differences are narrowing. Girls, now women, are willing to express their competitive spirits more openly today.

And certainly, there are executive women who are comfortable using brinksmanship skills. There are guys who are terrible at it too. Generally speaking, it's a question of practice. Boys, now men, got more of it over the course of their lifetimes. Women may arrive at the workplace and try it all for the first time.

My message here is that even if you never did it as a girl, you can still learn brinksmanship as a grown woman in the workplace. I viewed it like a role I was playing at the time. I was in plays in grade school and high school, so playing roles came naturally to me. If you ever participated in plays or theater growing up, you might come to embrace this rule fairly easily. But even if you didn't act, once you begin practicing the key moves of brinksmanship and get the payoff, it will come more naturally. Just keep practicing.

YOUR TURN

1. Before you begin a negotiation, learn from management what the "bottom" is. The bottom is the lowest you can go to get an approved, acceptable deal through your company. In personal matters such as negotiating salary, it is the lowest you are willing to go before you walk away from an offer.
2. The traditional negotiating style of start high, end in the middle is still the most tried and true.
3. When clients attempt to bully you or rant and rave, either conclude the session and explain you expect to be treated respectfully or hang around and make them crazy by showing

indifference. The "Are you through yet?" response works really well after they've put on an emotional show.

4. Never fence in negotiations because you risk puncture wounds. In other words, never get personal because you risk offending, and people have long memories.

5. The Walk Away is used when your opponents' bottom is too low to be acceptable to you. Be sure to stick to your guns, or the clients will keep moving the goal posts in their direction. The Walk Away can also be used to cut a session short if you need to send a message that your client is being grossly unreasonable.

6. The Bluff is a power challenge that you or your opponent can issue. Even if you are not comfortable bluffing yourself, go into the session with the knowledge that your opponent may be bluffing. Be sure to restate the benefits of the deal that are accruing to your client so you can build a wall against his or her bluff.

7. Pay attention to who holds the power in the room so you can focus on that person's concerns. Learning who has authority is a shortcut to more efficiently concluding business dealings. Also, pay attention to your client's workspace or office and what it reveals about him or her because it can be a bridge that will connect you two and help build rapport.

8. Look for physical mannerisms that tell what your opponent is thinking and feeling. Does he twist his hands in worry? Does he put his feet up on the desk in bravado? Does he feel more comfortable when you are eye to eye? These are all tells, all valuable bits of information you can use to your advantage.

9. Be aware of your own tells. Videotape yourself speaking or ask for feedback from a trusted colleague. Observe what you

are doing, physically, that may be giving your opponent an advantage. Do you have a tendency to tap your pencil or shuffle your papers? How do you act when under pressure? When you know your own tells, you can learn to control them.

10. Don't forget that the four key moves of brinksmanship are strategies you're employing to move forward in your career. Good gamers around you are using them too, so employing them puts you on the same playing field, with equal advantage.

11. When the going gets really tough, mentally whisper, "It's only a game, it's only a game," and that will help restore perspective to what is sometimes crazy and absurd behavior across the table.

Chapter 5

Build Your Fan Club

RULE 5: FAN CLUBS

The Game Context: A sports team gives us a great context in which to understand the role of fans. Not every athlete needs a fan club, but those who make team captain do.

The Business Setting: Growing a fan base is the work we do to gain team support for company initiatives as well as the forward motion of our careers. Attracting and maintaining team support is critical for any successful business leader, and it's trickier for women than men. We need the support of our management, our colleagues, and our teams to advance to the top.

LIKABILITY = BUSINESS SUCCESS

It's not just lonely at the top. For women, it can get pretty cold.

Take, for example, the experience of Marissa Mayer. Soon after ascending to the position of CEO at Yahoo!, Mayer announced she was pregnant. A few weeks later, when Yahoo! released its first earnings under her tenure, the headline in *USA Today* read: "Yahoo CEO's Pregnancy Overshadows Flat Revenue."

The article even mentioned that Mayer had at one time been involved romantically with Google founder Larry Page. It stopped short of suggesting that Page was the baby's father, but *still*. The story should have been about what the acclaimed new CEO was going to do to turn around Yahoo!'s fortunes, not about her pregnancy and former love life. This is where you have to ask, If the new CEO had been a man, would his former girlfriends be mentioned in an earnings report?

The world can be a brutal place for women as they move up the power ladder. To be successful, a woman on the rise needs more than a quick brain. She needs fans—people who believe in her and who are willing to stand by her, even when critics pass judgment or when she's down in the count.

But getting fans is a tricky process. It is not, as one would hope, a meritocracy. Fans do not flock only to the person who is best at the job—and that's true for men and women. Yes, fans look for a track record of success. But they also look for and gravitate to one more very important thing: likability.

Some women overlook the importance of likability in growing a support base. Far too many subscribe to the theory that rising to the top means being the best and that's all it takes.

So how do you boost your likability and build a fan base? There are many tactics at your disposal, but I'm going to focus on three important and often-overlooked ones in this chapter. The first is humor, and the second is building trust through soft power, and the third is the art of working well with men.

WHEN POSSIBLE, USE HUMOR

Call this the good humor solution.

No, not Good Humor as in the ice-cream truck. Good humor, as in using it as a leadership quality. Dwight Eisenhower said, "A sense of humor is part of the art of leadership, of getting along with people, of getting things done." When I mentor women, I always ask if they are comfortable laughing on the job, and I often see wariness and hear: "Not really. My colleagues won't take me as seriously if I cut up around them." There is a difference between being silly or immature and employing good humor. Silliness is giggling all the time, which is a nervous tell (see Chapter 4), usually indicating someone's lack of self-confidence. What I'm suggesting is good judgment in use of humor. Let it come naturally. It's about enjoying your job, rather than trying to be Chris Rock. Most of us couldn't pull that off if we tried.

Here's why we should turn to humor. Laughter and levity on the job lighten us, loosen us up as we face the daily stresses of work. The sports analog is grip pressure: A pitcher who holds a ball too tightly reduces spin on the ball, thus blunting his effectiveness against batters. Using a well-placed joke or good humor takes the tension out of the room when meetings are hitting a boiling point. It is a technique that diffuses stress. I once read a religious leader's opinion that in laughter the mind lets go and the heart opens. It also has medical impact: Laughter reduces inflammation in the arteries and increases good HDL cholesterol.

When people in management use humor, especially in a self-effacing way, it humanizes them and makes them more accessible to their teammates. It makes us more likable. Colleagues think, Well, they can laugh at themselves. Maybe I can do that too. Using humor helps us better relate to one another, to gain perspective as well as relieve stress.

Much has been written on this topic. One terrific book on the subject is *The Levity Effect: Why It Pays to Lighten Up* by Scott Christopher and Adrian Gostick. In it, the authors argue all the positives that result from lightening up at work. Good humor can get you hired. They researched 737 chief executives of major corporations and found that 98 percent would hire an applicant with a good sense of humor over one who seemed to lack one. The book also cites a survey of 1,000 workers conducted by the research firm Ipsos that found employees who laugh at work tend to stay on. Those whose bosses had an above-average sense of humor said there was more than a 90 percent chance they would stay on their job for more than one year, versus 77 percent who described their bosses as having an average or below-average sense of humor. Humor breeds job engagement and retention.

Many CEOs have embraced the role of humor in business success. When Twitter CEO Dick Costolo gave a commencement address at the University of Michigan, he spoke briefly about his work at the social media phenomenon but extensively about his days as an aspiring comedian in Chicago. Improv comedy, he told the graduates, taught him important lessons about risk taking and human connection that he went on to use—quite profitably—in the business world.

Robert J. Moore, CEO of RJMetrics, also sings the praises of humor skills for CEOs. Like Dick, he's an improv veteran. It started as a hobby, a way to exercise another part of his brain, but soon the skills he picked up learning to make people laugh made their way into his day job: active listening, team focus, going for the big laugh. They all made him a better CEO, Robert contends. Humor is an asset in leadership situations.

Someone who validated this for me was Frank Gardner. I first met Frank at a trade show in Anaheim in the early 1990s when I was still working with CNBC. He and Ken Lowe recruited me to join their startup HGTV. He was a corporate guy at Scripps, the parent of HGTV, and Ken's nascent HGTV unit would report in to him. Frank was a whirling dervish of energy and excitement as he pitched HGTV, since Ken had laryngitis that morning. Frank was equal parts dynamic, explosive, and hilarious. Between Ken's breadth of vision and Frank's style, I was sold.

When I came on board and the three of us began working together, Frank's first edict was to proclaim the No Asshole Rule.

"All right, by God, let's take a blood oath, if we're going to do this, start a business from scratch and have no reason to complain when we look back, let's make sure we don't hire any assholes! We can't hire anybody who's nuts. We need people who won't blow up the place!"

Frank didn't mean literally blow up the place. He meant blow up our culture. One of the first things those of us in the founding group did at HGTV, before the channel was even on the air, was to define the culture we wanted by agreeing upon our core values. Humor was one of them, along with more commonly used culture descriptors such as integrity and openness. But humor? Who had ever heard of humor being a core value in a company? It was in ours, and it taught me its importance. It would occur to me later how therapeutic laughing on the job felt, as the walls were closing in with the daily stresses of a startup.

How to Use Humor

There is an old Chinese saying: Blessed are those who can laugh at themselves, for they shall never cease to be entertained. The most powerful, engaging use of humor is the self-effacing or self-deprecating type, which means laughing at ourselves. I'm half Italian and half Greek, and those are two sides of crazy, especially the Greek side of my gene pool. You'll see some self-effacing barbs about my heritage in this book. In the workplace, research shows self-effacing humor makes a boss more likable. In a study conducted at Seattle University, undergraduates were presented with series of funny lines a CEO might use to introduce a new manager, Pat, to the team. Each one spotlights a slightly different use of humor. Take a look:

1. "I am so glad that Pat took this job, despite knowing all about *us!*"
2. "I am so glad that Pat took this job, despite knowing all about *you!*"
3. "I am so glad that Pat took this job, despite knowing all about *me!*"

Which punch line won the contest? The last one, in which the boss employs self-deprecating humor.

Another kind of humor is use of exaggeration. Frank Gardner, a great storyteller, told us about the process of buying Cinetel, a production facility we needed to jump-start HGTV's programming. Apparently he wore a blue wool suit on the summer day he went to close the deal. And here's how I heard him tell it, again and again. "It was about a thousand degrees out and I had splotches the size of India all over my body." This type of exaggeration stretches the truth, but its intent is never hurtful. Its intent is playful.

How *Not* to Use Humor

Steer clear of innuendo. And I'm speaking from experience.

We were in Paris in the mid-1990s, taking our charter advertising clients on a nice trip to thank them for their business. I was to kick off the welcome part of the meeting. At this point I had gotten more comfortable with trying humor to break the ice in meetings. I was doing my usual mental role-plays but couldn't arrive at a good ice breaker. Then it occurred to me, "When in Rome . . ." Wouldn't it be great if I said a few words in French to begin?

Except I didn't know any French, save a single line from the 1970s Motown tune "Lady Marmalade." So my introductory remarks went something like this: *"Bonjour. Voulez-vous coucher avec moi ce soir?"*

Turns out, I'd just asked our advertisers if they wanted to go to bed with me that night. Some clients familiar with the tune thought it was funny; some others didn't get it; some began libidinous mind wandering. The worst of it was the reaction on the part of the AV guys who were French natives, obviously fluent. I was pretty popular after that speech so I made a speedy retreat.

I was a green COO, but that's no excuse.

I'm not the only woman to have made that misstep. In her book,

Carly Fiorina tells a story about a team-building exercise meant to merge two sales forces. To show that her team was as tough as the new team they were merging with, she thought it would be funny to stuff some socks in the front of her trousers, then take the stage and declare that her group's "balls were as big as anyone's in the room."

While I didn't pretend to have a male body part, my opener in France was out of line. Men can take the risk with innuendo jokes—they never should, but they can. Women can't. Our reputations are more fragile, more easily tarnished. Moreover, who knows whether these kinds of jokes may encourage men in ways that are unsafe for women. For these reasons, stay away from jokes involving sexual innuendo. When I hear one from the guys, I shake my head and shame them with the Evil Eye.

TRUST, SOFT POWER, AND
HOW TO BUILD BOTH

When I was in my third year at HBO, I was recruited to join a hybrid sales and marketing team and do some experimental marketing with our customers to grow our collective revenues. This was a full-time job for about a year. The marketing required a lot of work on the part of our sales staff, our finance people, and our marketing department to pull it off successfully. Our pesky little group became an irritant for much of the HBO organization.

The group was headed up by an executive who was very smooth on her feet, and she didn't seem to mind taking all the arrows that were flying her way. After one really tough meeting I attended where an executive gave her a very hard time, I saw her shake her head and whisper, "That was my fault." Since that wasn't her normal MO, I asked her why. She said, "Because the day before he and I were in a meeting, and I didn't kiss his cheek in greeting."

This example may border on the absurd, but I tell it for two reasons. First, because she really believed that building a fan club was about cheek kisses, and she was a little bit right. How we treat others around us is noticed, especially as senior women. Recall we are scrutinized more than men. If we appear to be playing favorites within any team, ours or others, it can come back to bite us.

The second reason I include it is because she was mostly wrong. The best way to build team support within your organization is through building trust. When you build trust, you gain soft power.

Soft power is a phrase that came into vogue in the early 1990s to describe the political arena. A Harvard professor, Joseph Nye, wrote a couple of books about the preferability of soft power to political coercion. In politics it means attracting and persuading with a soft hand. Since then it's become applicable to business, and means influencing those who don't report to you. My longtime friend and colleague Dean Gilbert talked of it extensively when I spoke to him, because Silicon Valley has flat, broad organizational structures that pull people from various teams to work together. Soft power takes place when you influence those who sit with you on task forces and cross-functional teams. In using it, you are attempting to successfully navigate parts of your organization that you don't control. Hard power is telling your staffer what to do—and he will because you sign his paychecks. Soft power is much more, well, powerful, in organizations because most of us don't run the companies and therefore have very limited hard power.

Those with soft power are sometimes called influencers. They have a spiderweb of connections within their organizations and are trusted from many corners of the companies. Their work on teams boosts productivity of the whole organization. Influencers have used soft power to become a go-to, added-value person for their company.

Some of the best users of influence honed their skills in the world of video games. The video gamer mentality is often focused on social connectedness—the art of joining forces for a common purpose. Video gamers are influence builders in their own make-believe worlds, but those skills can translate profitably to business circles. Successful business gamers enjoy building up relationships all around them.

Some think of soft power as politicking, and they may criticize it as such. I argue that the foundation of soft power is *trust*, which is absent in politicking. Our management consultant Dr. Steve Martin loved his southernisms, and he would call politickers "top water bait." Since the closest I ever came to fishing was reading *The Old Man and the Sea*, I asked him to explain.

"Top water bait are used for shallow fishing, Susan," he said. "Those folks in business that are so shallow they never want to dive deep enough to know someone, well, in my book they're top water bait."

Top water bait think a kiss on the cheek will get them what they need.

Still more may see the process of soft power building as a waste of time—time better spent on revenue-generating activities. That's a huge misconception. If you asked a work colleague about me, they'd tell you I work quickly to complete things. I like to get to the period. I *hate* wasting time. Here are the reasons building soft power is not a waste of time:

- ◆ You will be more comfortable and effective in cross-functional environments.

- You will build a network of trust in the organization so you can more efficiently accomplish tasks.
- The network you build can help you advance your career because it is made up of people who know you and trust you.
- You may build lifelong friends from taking the time to get to know your peers, and how cool is that?

If you're a woman and you want to run a company someday, there are three things you need: competency, results, and trust. The first two are givens. To be at the top, you must be highly skilled, and back it with results. But that third element is trickier and often overlooked. It's this trust business that is the focus here. Business gurus, coaches, and consultants will say women are great at building trust. They'll say it's one of our strongest suits. I disagree. We may have all the empathetic and intuitive skills that would go into building trust, yet we fail to use those qualities at work because we're stymied by the usual societal methods and because *we don't want to take the time.* Men take the time to network at work; women generally don't. Again, we're talking about building trust in lateral team situations that we don't control, not with our own teams. With our teams we can spend the requisite time to know those folks well. Not so in cross-functional or task-force situations.

There are many ways to build trust and soft power at work. Ask your colleagues to breakfast or lunch. Learn about their families. If it's a woman and you are both married, suggest the four of you go to dinner. You can also do this with a man as a foursome, but it's a little dicier. Never ask a man to dinner without his spouse; that will send the wrong signal. Ask a woman to join your book club. Ask your peers to comment on something you're working on. Per Dean

Gilbert: "Men love to be asked their goddamn opinion." Genuinely use their feedback and later show them the final product, which incorporates some of their thinking (if it's worthwhile to include). Ask them to join a team you're assembling to think through an issue. If you learn that you both share some commonality of purpose outside of work, such as a charity, use that as a means to engage and build trust through time spent together on committees. Genuine friendships can come out of the time it takes to build this trust. My two lifelong closest male friends, Ken Lowe and Mark Hale, I met at SNI. We have stayed close for twenty years because we took the time to get to know one another.

Top-ranked women consistently show how soft power plays out in the business world. In 2012, Susan Wojcicki, senior vice president of Google and the highest ranking woman, was responsible for nearly 90 percent of the company's $50 billion in revenue. In March 2013, CEO Larry Page expanded Susan's portfolio to add their commerce unit to play a central role in Google's transition to mobile advertising. In early 2014, Larry gave her YouTube to run. When my friend Dean Gilbert worked with her at Google, he noted how she worked seamlessly with both men and women. She understood and built soft power all over the enterprise. She worked behind the scenes to build relationships, to "create a universe beyond the universe she owns and operates." She promoted scores of women and men who had worked for her, and many ended up going on to bigger jobs outside Google. She had the goodwill from promoting them, and she has stayed in touch with them. For those who still work at Google, she has an enormous sphere of goodwill throughout the organization because of all of those she promoted.

Not all soft power is built in the C-suite. There are everyday workplace courtesies that help build trust. I learned about these from Frank and Ken at SNI. In the beginning days of HGTV, I sent Frank, Ken's boss, an email in response to something and didn't copy Ken. He railed at me. "You always copy your boss if you're sending their boss an email!" I learned my lesson quickly after that. I probably looked like top water bait to Frank at the time. We hadn't built up enough of a relationship, and enough trust. Another common courtesy: If I wanted someone on a task force I was creating, I made sure I got permission from their supervisor, even if that supervisor was levels below me on the food chain. This wasn't just an email to the supervisor. I sat with them, explained my purpose, and asked if they could afford to have Jane or Jim spend x amount of time on this. In an organization, the person with the power has to be the person with the grace. Ken was big on walking-around time. Walk the floor. Look folks in the eye. Ask about their families.

This sort of personal matrix building is a long game. Beth Mooney, CEO of financial services giant KeyCorp, says one of the keys to her success is her longtime effort to maintain a cadre of supporters—she calls them her pit crew—throughout her career. These are people who have supported her along the way and offered her advice and counsel. Some are colleagues, others are coaches and mentors. As Beth moved up the food chain at KeyCorp, she made it a point to continue to reach out to these supporters. She thought of them in the context of a backup team (distinct from her everyday workplace team). But by maintaining contact, continually keeping the communication with her backup team going, Beth says she was able to maintain relationships that sustained her and helped her build her power base. That takes time and effort, but there's no question it's an investment that pays off.

I've seen that time and again in my own work. David Zaslav,

currently CEO of Discovery Communications, and I worked at CNBC together, he at corporate HQ and I in the Detroit regional office. He and I competed for jobs and collaborated on deals. I'd met his wife, Pam, and knew about his kids. He always asked after my family too. We built mutual trust. We've stayed in touch over the years, and when I began consulting, I needed a favor with a client. In a day he'd taken care of it. This is an ideal example of building soft power. You stay connected even when you're in a competitive situation with someone during portions of your career.

To put a fine point on it, the difference between politicking and building trust is that the former is all about you, what can *you* gain from the action. The latter is about reciprocity. Sure, you'll need to call on those you've built soft power with, but you'll also be there for them when they need you.

WORKING WITH MEN

Sometimes, you just have to acknowledge that men are different. And knowing how to work with them to build trust and support is a key to success.

Meetings in the Restroom

For societal and anatomical reasons, women don't have ready access to the men's restroom. That creates a big hassle with long lines in theater and concert intermissions. It's also a business problem. A lot goes on in men's restrooms that we're not a part of. I've been ambushed plenty of times by the phenomenon of the "restroom pre-meeting"—we get in a conference room to discuss the agenda, and the outcomes have already been decided. How did this happen? It happened because the guys took a bathroom break before the meeting, discussed their upcoming meeting issues, strolled in, and had all the answers.

While men can have their meetings in the restroom, on the golf course, at the sports bar, and in other male-dominated social settings, women have more limited, acceptable ways to build relationships with men. It's easier for men to build their own fan clubs with other men because they have more opportunities to interact in a social/business setting. Often they are in situations that are not welcoming to women. They have more time to bond, among themselves and without women around. Women are traditionally shut out of many of the male-bonding scenarios. But the simple truth is this: To advance in our companies we have to figure this out.

You find the playing field full of men as you rise. They are colleagues; they are bosses. Some become friends, if you're lucky. You need their support as colleagues and bosses for promotions and plum assignments. You need their emotional trust and support as friends to make work more satisfying. You need them in your fan club.

Men have some inherent advantages over us because they *are* men; to a large extent corporate business has been their turf. It was put well by Amy Schulman, former executive vice president at Pfizer, when she said in an interview that coming into an environment dominated by men is like learning a new language and they are speaking the native tongue. Whoever owns the language wins the conversation.

There are also subtle and often unconscious biases, call them blind spots, that prevail in business when women and men are considered for promotions. It's like the story of the two little fish by David Foster Wallace:

> *There are these two young fish swimming along and they happened to meet an older fish swimming the other way, who nods at them and says, "Morning, boys. How's the water?" And the two young fish swim on for a bit, and then eventually one of them looks over the other and goes, "What the hell is water?"*

The moral of this little story? When you're too close to something (or in this case, swimming in it), it's easy to have blind spots.

Unconscious bias, or the implicit preference for a certain group that influences workplace decisions, is a hot topic in HR circles. Training programs are springing up all over the country to help employees and supervisors recognize and better deal with these. For women, the blind spots that put men ahead of them in the promotional queue are a big part of these trainings.

Alice Schroeder began her career as a CPA in Houston. She worked her way up in finance to Wall Street and was ultimately elevated to managing director at Morgan Stanley. Along the way she covered an insurance business that Warren Buffett acquired and had the vision to follow Warren's stock, even though it wasn't actively traded and even though he was more of a recluse at that time. To this day it dumbfounds her that other brokerage firms did not follow Berkshire, a Fortune 20 company. Ultimately, she wrote the *New York Times* bestseller *The Snowball: Warren Buffett and the Business of Life*, chronicling Warren Buffett's life. Today Alice sits on several corporate boards, including Prudential (PLC), a $60 billion company. She shares one of her first perceptions about working within a male-dominated culture:

Of course, it is hard for all institutions to see themselves objectively and dispassionately. The Wall Street business culture is very specific and defined, and the people in that ecosystem—for the most part men—believe it's a meritocracy. Many of them would disagree if you told them it is not a women-friendly environment, there are thick glass ceilings that create institutional barriers for women, and there is considerable pressure for women to behave like men. When you see how few women have gotten into very senior roles, and the hurdles the women who've succeeded on Wall Street have had to leap to get those roles, ultimately, if they don't succeed, it's not the women that are the problem.

It's not just a Wall Street problem. I saw this myself in cable TV programming, where even a Fortune 46 company like Comcast Communications has only one woman in its most senior ranks. And Anne-Marie Slaughter worked for Secretary of State Hillary Clinton and has commented often about the Washington political and government world being a close-knit boys' club.

Just knowing that many of the biases against women are unconscious may be helpful in comprehending why this still goes on in the workplace. Having said that, women are left with the issue of how to advance when men are making most of the promotional decisions.

Work Well with Captains of Industry

Captains of industry dot the business landscape. They're the richest and most powerful. They run the largest companies and sit on the most elite boards. Some have protected and defended the male business hierarchy either consciously or unconsciously for generations.

During your career you may work with such captains. Some of you will emerge as captains too, and working with them is good training for that.

Alice shares this:

My first meeting with Warren Buffett took place flying on his private jet out to Omaha and doing the interview on the airplane. A man as brilliant as him was not oblivious to the impact it would have on someone to put someone who's never flown on a private jet on a Gulfstream 4 with a flight attendant who offers to cook them lunch. What better setting to convey authority, power, and credibility.

One reason that Warren took to Alice, she believes, was because she didn't misuse her access to him, which included his direct phone number. She rarely called him and went to see him only about once a year. Because she was respectful of his time, he saw that her engagements with him came from a place of genuine interest in his business. He came to trust her and later approached her to write *The Snowball.*

I became one of the handful of people that Warren Buffett wanted to spend his time with, partly because I wasn't conniving. Like many rich and famous people, he is constantly being approached by an army of people who want things from him. Warren handles these people deftly; it's one of his best talents. I was in the other group, one of those who didn't ask for anything, which he values. It's a relief for him to get a break from constantly constructing warm-sounding ways to say no. So that was part of how our relationship developed.

Alice also came to know Bill Gates through her friendship with Warren. "Bill cannot go in public without being besieged. Although he's as gracious as can be toward every person who addresses him, there's usually been fifty before them. I have actually gone through a buffet line for Bill because he can't get his own food in peace."

At this point you may be saying, Well, so what? I'd *love* to have those problems. Maybe. But I include these stories to point out that these men just want human, authentic interaction. As Alice says, "They oversleep, they get colds, they have bad days and good days like everyone else. They're not ordinary people, but they're *human*." This attitude starts with seeing them as real people who are being yanked in a million different directions all of the time, who have families, and worries, and enormous demands made of them. If you can be sincere, authentic, and respectful of their time, you can build trust.

Engage Constructively

The tried-and-true, never-fail way to work effectively with men is through constructive engagement. Simply put, always add value to a meeting or one-on-one engagement with a man, or woman, or team. Make it a habit. Arrive prepared and thoughtful about the meeting's topic. Demonstrate that you are intellectually credible. Alice explains:

I think that building your career strategy around yourself is less likely to work than building your strategy around making the results of your work amazing. If someone tells you to make a widget, you can decide that your widget is going to be ten times better than any widget that has ever been made. I don't pay much attention to how

*things have been done by other people. I think, What is the absolute
best way that I could do this and make it amazing?*

Alice's thinking is the foundation of constructive engagement:
Add unique value wherever you can. Advancement will most likely
come from men, since that's the playing field above you, and promotions will come when you constructively engage with them. Bring
a new perspective. Help build consensus in meetings. Work for win–
wins. Debate a point with artful assertiveness. Try not to take it
personally if someone debates back. Some people just like to hear
the sound of their own voice. Understand your consumer and the
other business drivers. You can do these things well if you've done
your homework through learning and practice. After every engagement the right question to ask is never, Do I belong here? It is, Have
I added value here?

Manage Confrontation

Problems don't go away if you ignore them. They just get bigger. A
way to work effectively with men is to be willing to manage confrontation, and as quickly as possible. Men handle confrontation
more readily than women. Competition and confrontation are two
sides of the same coin. To win you will need to confront, so you must
practice it as men have.

Let's say you're in the situation of having beaten a man out of a
job. You got the promotion, he didn't. This is a really good thing,
right? Yes and no. You need to ask, Can the guy who lost hurt you
in the workplace as he now works for you? Can he sabotage you?
The best thing to do is to walk into his office as soon as you both
are given the news, to close the door, and to confront him. Tell him

very plainly that you won this round, but you want and need him to be on your team. Tell him what you find enriching about his work and how it will benefit you and the team. (This assumes you do want to work with him.) It's human nature for all of us to like hearing good things when our egos are bruised. You are showing understanding and empathy by doing this. Recall that he lost the round. Some understanding goes a long way.

And if the flip side of that happens, and you lose out to a man, reach out to him and congratulate him. He'll remember that about you and may be able to help you with advancement in the future.

Build Rapport

On the sports field, trash talk is common. It goes on all the time as players use it to get into the other guy's head. It's a good thing pro basketball courts and football fields aren't miked, because the trash talk there wouldn't be suitable for children. Between businessmen, it is how they playfully tease and cut one another down. You may walk into a meeting and one guy remarks to another: "Nice haircut." Or, "Nice tie." You know in both cases the guy means it as a playful insult. And the bad-hair or bad-tie guy gets it. He cuts down the other guy in some way. Then they both laugh and probably go to lunch after the meeting.

For women, some form of modified trash talk teasing is OK, but you can't ever get too personal with men. I've teased colleagues about clothes, but never hair. We women don't like being teased about our hair; neither do guys (by women; as mentioned, it seems to be fine between men). Never, ever tease about family matters. Saying something like "I saw your wife yesterday. Did she have a nose job?" just wouldn't work. I could get into the rhythm of some good-hearted teasing with my male colleagues as long as it stayed light and was never personal.

This book is all about how sports are analogous to business in many ways. That's not a surprise, given that men have been the purveyors of both for centuries. Conversing about sports does provide a connector, a bridge for knowing men better. If you enjoy some particular sport, you can ask your colleague if he likes it too or has played it. You don't need to know as much about it as him. If you enjoy it, that's enough. Maybe you're a runner and your colleague is too. For sports to work as a shared topic you need to have genuine interest. Otherwise the conversation will be stilted and *not* genuine.

Another area of common personal interest might be vacation spots you've found with your family that you want to share. I've worked with many colleagues whose personal time was spent primarily on travel. Knowing this, you can share your own travel adventures with them. That's another good source of connection.

Finally, family may be the best connector. Asking what's going on with the kids is a great opener whenever there are, in fact, kids.

YOUR TURN

1. Dial down your serious, perfectionist demeanor. Perfectionism is rarely called for at work. In most places, 90 percent precision is better than 100 percent because speed takes precedence over unimportant details, which typically make up that last 10 percent.
2. There are lots of types of humor, but the most effective is if you can lighten up and laugh at yourself. It humanizes you to your colleagues.

3. If you're addressing a group, it helps to break the ice with some humor. If this makes you nervous, do mental role-plays and rehearsals.

4. Building soft power takes time. There are no shortcuts. Taking the time will be worth it as you will grow relationships of mutual trust.

5. In working with people of influence, use your insight, empathy, and good listening skills to see beyond the glitz of their lives. If you are authentic, and not just out to get something from them, you can build trust over time.

6. With men, ways of building trust are handling confrontation quickly and directly, staying in frequent contact with those you promote, and finding connectors you might have in common (such as sports, travel, and family).

Chapter 6

Practice, Practice, Practice

RULE 6: PRACTICE, PRACTICE, PRACTICE

The Game Context: Practice is the work you do that gets you no applause but prepares you for the moment when the game's on the line. From laps to reps to watching the tapes in the locker room, practice is what we do all week so that we're at our best at game time. We develop muscle memory and winning skills that become second nature to us because we practice them. If conditioning is the skill level we must acquire, then practice is the path that gets us there.

The Business Setting: In business, as in sports, there is a difference between game day and practice time. Practice encompasses the smaller moments that may seem less significant but, woven together, prepare you for important career opportunities to stand out and to be successful. When you face an opponent in any business situation—a negotiation, a competition for a plum assignment, a shot at a promotion—your chances of success often hinge on how well you execute under pressure. It's not a time to rely on luck. Good execution develops through practice, and success follows. While you need baseline talent, it's the willingness to learn and then practice new skills that allow you to advance.

PUTTING IN YOUR 10,000 HOURS

In his book *Outliers: The Story of Success,* author Malcolm Gladwell cites the "10,000-Hour Rule"—the key to success in any field is a matter of practicing for 10,000 hours. That's a lot of hours. While not everyone I know embraces that math, the concept of practice is one I've heard many times. Ken Lowe, chairman and CEO of Scripps Networks Interactive, the largest producer of lifestyle programming networks, offers a crucial piece of advice:

> *Practice, practice, practice. It's critically important. The one thing you do learn in sports early is repetition. Let's do it again. This was Vince Lombardi's line. "We're going to be here all night, guys, until you get this down." The good thing about that is repetition does indeed, in any endeavor, build muscle memory. So when you're leading a group, when you're meeting challenges, when things become stressful, repetition allows you to not think so much.*

Ken was talking about having such a deep and rich understanding of your job that you could almost intuitively perform it. Earlier in this book I addressed the issue of conditioning—the skills needed for success. Practice is what moves you along the continuum and toward the career goals you've set for yourself. Learning new skills is critical. But to make it all happen—to get from good to great—you need to take every opportunity to get out there and practice.

As a newly minted HBO salesperson, I figured the best way to be successful was to understand how my customers, the cable operators, thought. If I could learn what was on their minds, get into their heads a bit, I could find some bridge or some connection to them. In so doing, I could sell them not only what I *wanted* to sell them but also what they *needed*. What a concept.

Breaking things down into little steps has always been the easiest way for me to move toward a goal. My first step was to get *ample time* with the potential client. I could buy him lunch. But I needed more than an hour and I needed more than social talk. I had to understand his needs. So when I scheduled my meeting with the client in Quincy, Illinois, in the dead of winter, I asked him if I could climb poles when I got there. For many, cable TV comes into your home from wires that are strung on telephone poles. To string the cable, the system engineers have to climb up the poles and do their work there. My offer to climb poles was an offer to learn his business. That got his attention. The game was on.

When I arrived, he was ready for me. He handed over all the gear: the gloves, the clips, the hardhat. Up a phone pole I went with him, and when we got to the top, it was a sight to behold. We had a panoramic view of his lovely little town from up there. He spent time explaining the nuances of stringing together his community. Then we climbed down.

I asked to go into their "headend"—the large, climate-controlled room inside their offices where all of the modulators and satellite receiving equipment are kept. It was a chance for us to discuss the equipment and its uses, which we did.

Why did I bother with all this? My clients were engineers, while I was an advertising major. We had what you might call a gap, and it was up to me (salesperson) to close it. So I climbed poles, studied his gear, and could then understand enough to connect with him. *I could ask the right questions.* I could be more than some young woman with a bag of movies, sports, and specials to sell. I did the additional work so that I could come to the table not as an outsider trying to make a sale but as someone who had demonstrated an interest in selling him solutions. The proverbial win–win. I practiced learning his business. It made me better able to understand what he needed and refine my approach. With those extra hours of practicing under my belt, I took him to lunch and made the sale.

Practice is all about the various ways we keep learning, keep improving, to eventually master our jobs. Through preparation and repetitions of practice where needed, we acquire the competency and credibility to deliver big results. In this chapter, I examine practice from three enriching perspectives: There is active, on-the-job practice (like climbing poles), and the more cerebral kind, which I call mental practice. Next, we'll look at cross-training practice, which broadens our skill sets.

ACTIVE PRACTICE

Theodore "Tim" Solso is a good example of active practice. He became non-executive chairman of General Motors in early 2014. He didn't just sit in the boardroom and preside over meetings. Just days after being elected, Tim was walking the Chevy factory production lines and touring GM's design center and R&D labs. Active practice involves everything from walking factory floors, as Tim did, to climbing poles, to participating in training programs. It includes attending trade shows and walking the floor. It could mean tasting product samples for a new food item your company is producing. It can mean rehearsals you do with your team so you can be top notch in an important meeting or client pitch. All of this practice is preparation for mastering your job or understanding your customers better so you can problem solve. All of these forms of practice enrich you and prepare you to win big.

I'm a fan of rehearsals and role-plays. They're great for team building, and they ensure that everyone is on the same page with the messaging you want to deliver. Often you have only one shot to win, and a lot is riding on how you perform at a given moment in time. Inevitably, there is a detail or two that hasn't been thought through, and rehearsals help you vet them. You and your team can role-play how various scenarios should be handled, depending on what you might hear in your meeting. Rehearsals help you arrive with professional polish as you face your audience. They're great training sessions for your staff. Your goal is to present as one smooth, composed voice, ready to hit it out of the park.

Another great team-building and team-learning experience is to do postscript meetings after your big moment. What did you do right? What could you have done differently? Were there any blind-side tackles that took you out of the game, if even momentarily? Postscripts are a good habit to get into for both your education as well as the team's.

Role-plays and rehearsals can occur with just two people or they can occur with eight or ten. They can be preparation for a board meeting or help you garner agreement on an everyday work issue that's keeping you from maximizing your performance. They allow you to better manage the outcomes of any situation because you can anticipate how people will respond when you put yourself in their shoes. Envisioning their questions and concerns in this safe setting, you're prepared to address them when the real meeting convenes. Having some control over outcomes builds confidence.

MENTAL PRACTICE

Practice often comes down to watching the tape.

Professional athletes spend most of their time practicing so that when game time comes, they're ready. Practice does not just take place on the field. A big part of practicing is watching tape of the opposing team's previous games and learning from them how to engage the competition effectively. In the NFL, for example, each team has to send its last three game films to its next opponent exactly one week before they play. Each sport has its own rules and customs. The coaches and players in all these sports look at these and think, How did that basketball guard manage to spot up and shoot when being pressed? How can that quarterback evade the rush and successfully complete passes? What offensive strategies does this team employ to win time after time, and how can we respond to that at game time? The actual practice of watching the tape helps players and coaches project how to win.

Albert Einstein once said, "Education is not the learning of many facts but the training of the mind to think." Mental practice is all of the ways to engage our brains in the pursuit of knowledge so that we can better do our jobs. If we are willing to apply our minds to learning, we can keep them stretched, agile, and stimulated. It's why many retirees stay engaged in puzzles and word games of different sorts. Studies have been done on memory and thinking, and those who did mentally stimulating things from childhood on had a slower rate of memory decline than those who weren't mentally active.

In 2013, there was a panel for senior media execs. Ken was there, and he shared this story:

I think it's important that you have this healthy curiosity. I was just at a conference, and there was a panel with Rupert Murdoch, Barry Diller, and John Malone. Charlie Rose asked them at the end, What keeps you guys going? Why are you still out there? And here are these guys in their seventies and eighties, and they all said the same word: discovery. They can't wait to discover what else is out there, what other deals are out there, how the media business will develop. I thought to myself, That's a great line. Ask a young person today, What drives you? And we hope they'll say discovering new ways to do business, discovering how we do business, discovering everything within the organization.

The starting point of engaging in mental practice is reading. You need to continue to take the time to learn more about your business by reading. Your industry will have trade magazines and journals and websites that cover the happenings in your field. Here's where you can learn trends and industry developments. Business magazines like *Forbes* and *Fortune* and newspapers like the *Wall Street Journal* capture general business trends that provide for a bigger picture beyond your specific industry. *Advertising Age*, one of my favorites, covers new products and the marketing that goes into them as well as consumer trends. Read them in the paper or online form. And here's the win: This kind of reading helps us connect the dots between consumer behavior and business trends, which in turn helps us be better problem solvers.

"I can't read enough when it comes to consumer research trends," Ken said.

I mean I just devour it. I love what goes on in society. So that's part of my preparation. I read about five papers daily. It goes back to connecting the dots. If this is happening here, wait a minute, this is something that needs to be recognized. I just read this article where they sold more refrigerators than they have ever sold in the history of selling refrigerators. Well, what does that mean? And then another article comes along that says there's this whole push to organic food. So all of a sudden, people are upgrading their refrigerators because there are new compartments to store organic foods and that's going to change the way people market and sell appliances and groceries. Just connecting the dots.

My ninety-six-year-old aunt, Rachel Hessen, was the second female to be named vice president at Revlon when she was made head of new product development, sales, and marketing for beauty products in 1970. Aunt Ray never made it past ninth grade, but that didn't limit her. She has a clear, articulate way of speaking, which she learned from reading practice. She read anything she could get her hands on to improve her vocabulary so that she could win in the workplace, and boy did she ever.

Plan B's and Mental Role-Plays

Now let's talk about the power of solo role-plays.

Athletes, like businesspeople, often mentally project a future competition and visualize how they could win it. Victor Espinoza, jockey of 2014 Kentucky Derby and Preakness Stakes winner California Chrome, said in an interview that he heard the coaching voice of his older brother in his head before the Preakness, whispering to use his head, not his soft hands, to think his way through how to best ride the horse for the win. By envisioning the challenges he could face in the race and how best to counter them, he went on to win the Preakness.

You should do role-plays and rehearsals with teammates, but you should also do them by yourself. Mental practice includes taking the time to think through strategies and approaches to problems before presenting them. This can be especially true with disruptive issues you need to prevail on so you can do a course correction or bring in new resources. That preparation will also add confidence because you've envisioned ahead of time the kinds of questions and challenges you might face.

But we win some, and we lose some. What did things look like if all didn't go according to plan? Because guess what? It often doesn't. When you face rejection, have a Plan B.

A way to introduce Plan B's looks something like this: You have already thought through an alternative way to solve the problem that's on the table, so that's just what you say. "OK, I understand why you've got the concerns you've stated [ceding a point]. Here's another way we can solve our problem." By giving them a point for their volley your way, it relieves a little tension in the room and opens your colleague(s) up to actively listen, not just tune you out.

Plan B's can give you more confidence. It starts with a healthy cynicism about your initial plans and strategies. You should assume you'll need a backup plan and actually prepare one. Having a Plan B gives you confidence to keep pushing because you've come prepared for whatever may roll your way.

Having said all this, I didn't always voice my Plan B's. For women to try to win points, it's all about finesse. Men can bully their points home, but if women try to do that by controlling the floor at meetings, we can quickly lose the precious support of colleagues. We become one of those B-words. We need to make judgment calls about whether we should voice our backup plans if we lose the first round. Sometimes it's best—when the win isn't a big enough deal to fight for—to fold your hand and not press on. I still recall moderating a panel with Ellen Kullman, chairman and CEO of DuPont, when she told the audience, "You don't have to prove you're the smartest person in the room." Good collaborators recognize the nuances of when to fight and when to concede. It's that old adage about winning the battle but losing the war. It's more important that you live to fight another day.

Efficient Ways to Practice

Before you tell me you have no time for mental practice, let's talk about learning efficiency. Because women are the busiest creatures on earth, there are ways we can be efficient about our learning. I have absorbed plenty in one trip to a trade show by walking the floor and talking to people. In two days of sitting in on panels, reading the propaganda dispensed there, and just walking around, I come back armed with knowledge that would allow me to cook up strategies to help my company. This is speed learning; it takes only a day or two. It can be expensive for your company to send you to these events if your job doesn't require attending, but you should still ask to attend at least once. Prepare your pitch. Explain what the company gets out of it—their win is an employee with more industry knowledge who can then add more value to the organization. All they can say is no. If they do say no, next year ask again.

If you travel often, take industry reading with you instead of your latest fun novel. You can read the novel at night. When you are reading, learn to speed-read by skimming and skipping through stories not relevant to your company or your industry.

If you manage people, have your team cook up strategies and Plan B's so that it's not all on you. It's how *they* learn.

The goal of mental practice is not to earn a PhD in business or to usurp family time. The goal is good use of your time and efficient learning wherever possible.

CROSS-TRAINING PRACTICE

In 2014, Ronee Hagen retired as CEO of Polymer Group, a multibillion-dollar company. She raised kids, then started her own business, and at fifty years of age, she joined the corporate world. She did a lot of zigging and zagging, bobbing and weaving in her career. She now serves on corporate boards, a third work chapter in her life.

Perhaps the hardest thing to grasp in a career is that there will be zigs and zags. Good businesspeople like speed. We want results. Setting up one's career for the best results takes time and openness to new roles that may come along. Practice in this context, then, means jobs that don't necessarily come with a bigger title but always come with new opportunities for growth and learning.

In my work experience I saw people move laterally much more frequently than making a straight line up to the corner suite. I was one of those. I created a career roadmap when I got out of school, and most of it didn't happen the way I thought. But interestingly, each decade brought significant growth. In my twenties I ran around as a solo salesperson making my way but also took on a lateral job in sales and marketing to learn more about marketing. By thirty, I was in sales management, supervising teams of people. This brought huge development in management skills, budgets and expense management, legal discipline, and emotional maturity. Just shy of forty, I was made COO. I wasn't yet ready to be HGTV's COO, but I said yes because I trusted those around me—my inside and outside networks—to help me do this job, to grow into it. As we evolved HGTV we grew into SNI, a multiple-network programmer, which allowed for additional cross-training. I took on several lateral moves at SNI as a part of broadening there.

Statistics from the Bureau of Labor Statistics show that, as of 2010, the average American had an average of eleven jobs from the age of eighteen to forty-six. We have to get out of our minds the belief that there's no such thing as lateral growth. It's plentiful! If you look around your organization, these opportunities exist in the form of task-force work, cross-functional teams, and movements into jobs in a different department. If you're willing to take on these assignments, or are willing to stay with your job as it morphs into something new and different, it's remarkable how such experience will broaden out your skill base.

Ursula Burns, CEO of Xerox, started as an engineer and then moved to become executive assistant to the president of marketing, before making her climb to CEO. Anne Sweeney, recently retired co-chair of Disney Media Networks and president of Disney/ABC Television Group, made a wholesale change from teacher to work in children's programming, which began her stellar ascent to her massive job of running a media empire. Kathleen Finch, now holding a powerful role at SNI, ran programming for three of the six SNI brands before her role as president of the home category.

Ken Lowe did lateral moves in the film business before he shifted industries. He recalls:

> *I thought I'd be directing films when I was in college, and so I did a little bit of everything. I set up lighting, developed the film, processed the film. I wasn't always the shooter, the editor, or the director. And on the surface this probably sounds romantic, Boy, that's a great Hollywood story. Look how he started and where he is today. But it was hardly that.*

He tells us why it's smart:

> *If you really want to know how an organization works, you need to get in the guts of it. There are too many times today where people come in and say, "I've got my degree and I will work only in this level, I'll do only this or that." The best is to learn a place from the inside out. And then when you end up running it or running a department, you have this experience and can say, "You know what? I know what goes on in those production meetings because I used to run them, and that's just not right." It gives you background understanding of an organization or an industry you might be in, that many times young people miss. They miss the richness of doing different roles and understanding really what it takes to run a company.*

We are better equipped to take executive roles if we're willing to break out of our specialty silos. By gaining a wider set of skills, we begin to see the playing field as a part of a bigger, broader picture of business, and of life. In *Composing a Life*, Mary Catherine Bateson profiled five highly productive women whose ambitions were constantly refocused on new goals and possibilities. They became proficient at adapting and saw all of life as a creative process, including their work. She argues that learning to adapt helped these women overcome career obstacles and live a more fluid life.

I have always had sales responsibility, but in the early career days it was *all* I had, so I couldn't understand how the financial and legal functions were interwoven in what I did every day. Once I was given a departmental budget, I began to understand the need for accountability to the company for something other than revenues. When I added new business development, I saw that we could make money from activities other than what the sales forces brought in. International gave me the broadest view of all, recognizing that our offerings had to fit into new cultures, and we had to learn and respect these cultures if we wanted any success overseas. All of these jobs helped me strategically connect the dots, and unbeknownst to me at the time, they helped prepare me for the chief operating role I would later take on.

Harvard professor Joseph L. Bower argues it takes a long while to develop future business leaders, and companies have a responsibility to their people to give them the time to grow. He argues companies need to balance short-term financial goals with the slower-paced practice of developing new talent. Wharton School professor Peter Cappelli says that not only do companies need to have the patience to grow their leaders but they need to provide the opportunities for people to grow. Without opportunities, workers grow frustrated. It is all too common a situation, he says.

Some companies recognize the need for this horizontal learning. Bristol-Myers Squibb's communications chief, Bob Zito, encourages his staff to change their jobs frequently. His goal: keep people excited, and nimble.

Amy Miles is an unusual talent because she just had one specialty area, finance, before she became CEO of Regal in 2009. Given that business speaks in the language of finance, a financial background is one of the few areas that alone can be preparatory for a future CEO role. Still, she said there was no way she would have been ready to take on the CEO role if she hadn't cross-trained.

"It wasn't a slam dunk," she said of getting the job. "The board said you're the potential candidate, but here are some things you need to do to get ready for that next role. I had to spend a lot more time with our operations department, and on teams that were operations led versus finance led, to get a better understanding of what happens in the theaters. I had to spend a lot more time with our film department, to get a better understanding of how that piece of our business works not just from a financial perspective but from a strategic perspective."

BE MEMORABLE

It's a good thing to be memorable at work. Someone taking note of your good work can lead to bigger career opportunities. But, like anything else you want to do well, it takes hours of practice time (often in obscurity) so that when the big moment comes, you're ready.

What are some ways to become memorable? If you are willing to take on and practice new skills through new assignments, like I did morphing from salesperson to faux lawyer, you will distinguish yourself. You will be thought of as wanting to broaden, to learn more, and most important, to add more value to the company. Sometimes that means taking on assignments that others don't want. It's pretty safe to say that the work I was doing with these deal negotiations no one else wanted to do. They were horribly contentious, long-winded affairs that could make a saint pull her hair out. But by being willing to keep at it and to transform my skills to adjust to the changing landscape, I stood apart from others in companies where I worked.

Ronee Hagen agrees. "I love that quote, 'Don't be agreeable, be memorable.' I think that if you really are serious about getting ahead, you do have to distinguish yourself, and distinguishing yourself doesn't mean just beating the person next to you. It means bringing a greater value to the company than perhaps somebody else does, and really having an expertise that is recognized, and then leveraging that to bigger, broader positions. It means sometimes going outside your comfort zone. But if you're serious about getting ahead, the idea of sitting there and just working hard and being a very good corporate controller or whatever it is you are, well, that's what you're paid to do. Kind of the minimum expectation. How do you distinguish yourself?"

Through active and mental practice and by cross-training opportunities, you will stand apart on the playing field. You'll be memorable to those who can make a difference in your career.

YOUR TURN

1. Take the time to really practice job-learning skills. It takes both the active and mental practice routines that will help you to grow in your job.
2. Determine when you've adequately practiced for an engagement, then find ways to relax away from the material. Deep, calm breathing before an engagement can help settle you.

3. Do as many mental role-plays as needed to think through what objections might surface and how you would address them. Rehearse as often as needed with staff before presenting material and do collective role-plays.

4. With strategic operations or client work, always have a Plan B strategy in your back pocket in case you encounter a wall of resistance to your first approach. Pick and choose your battles carefully, based on how high the stakes are for you and your company.

5. Practice through reading as well as doing. Reading leads to knowledge. Subscribe to industry trades and general business resources either online or in paper form.

6. Consider assigning a team member as industry expert and have that person report on current trends to the team, which will augment your own learning. Rotate the position over time so everyone has the opportunity to learn and report.

7. Aggressively seek to work in cross-functional teams and task forces to broaden your knowledge.

8. Be open to lateral moves to broaden your scope of learning, but seek these in line work, not support work.

9. Consider taking unpopular line jobs or tasks that will differentiate you from your peers.

10. Keep your eyes open to any morphing of your job duties and get a head start on learning the needed new skills. Be sure your supervisor knows you want this new learning—perhaps the company will pay for it.

Chapter 7

Suit Up

RULE 7: UNIFORM REQUIREMENTS

The Game Context: Every team has a uniform. Uniforms play an important role in signaling the side you're playing for. Dressing like you're not respectful of the uniform can impact how you're perceived in any competition.

The Business Setting: Like any high-profile athlete, your attire is part of your brand. It makes a statement about how seriously you take your role in the enterprise.

A MEMORABLE WARDROBE
MALFUNCTION

I still remember what I wore my first day at HBO—it was a tangerine blazer. This color would have worked well if I were a food group, but not if I wanted to meld with the chic Ivy League crowd that HBO seemed to hire. My colleagues all looked elegant; I looked like Rodney Dangerfield's daughter. Back then it seemed every morning was like a bad hair day: My clothes were uncooperative and unmanageable. I had to learn how to tame my wardrobe, and it took some practice.

By the time I was COO of HGTV, I'd learned to become a more neutral, classic dresser. I was feeling good about how my taste in clothes had evolved. One spring night, I was asked to say a few words to our advertisers at an event at New York City's Rainbow Room. It was a very high-end affair. I had been running late that day, so I sped through a clothing change at my hotel, sprinted over to the venue, said a few quick hellos, and dashed up and grabbed the mike to speak. In the midst of my remarks I happened to glance down.

My skirt was on backward. Completely backward—with the zipper teeth gleaming in the spotlights. And no, this wasn't one of those times when you could smile and pretend that was how the thing should be worn. It was on backward, clearly.

I was thrown completely off track. I quickly summed up my remarks, got down from the stage, and headed straight for the restroom, doing what I could to recover from this fumble.

UNIFORMS MATTER

Dressing is an important aspect of gamesmanship. You need to wear a neat, clean uniform if you want to be chosen to take the field. If it's messy or unkempt—or backward—you could get benched and have to work yourself back into the game. As a woman, what you wear will be observed and scrutinized. It's the outer layer of your overall package, which includes your brainpower, composure, communication skills, and fan club. It may be the easiest thing to get wrong, but the good news is it's also the easiest thing to get right.

If you are already a neutral, classic dresser, who doesn't clang with jewelry, and who likes clothing that doesn't draw attention to your excellent (or not-so-excellent) figure, then this chapter is not for you.

But if you're like me—if you can envision getting to a public speaking engagement with your skirt on backward—you might need a little practice with this rule, so read on.

The Everyday Uniform

What you wear to work every day is part of your workplace brand. It's the message that comes across before you open your mouth to speak.

I have one fundamental rule for women when it comes to the everyday uniform: Don't dress provocatively.

There are many ways this can be problematic for a women but not for a man. There is no such thing as a provocative workplace outfit for a man. If he has unbuttoned the top three buttons of his shirt, he is probably one of my Greek relatives. No one really cares; they may think it is inappropriate, but not provocative. If a woman does this, it can spell disaster.

Your goal in dressing is not to be voted Miss January. You can never forget that men are in abundance as you move into more senior roles. They notice how you dress. If they see anything that might be construed as suggestive or inappropriate attire, they will either be uncomfortable around you, or get the wrong idea and make a play for you. Or they may just band together and gossip about you. Clearly, none of these outcomes is desirable.

And sometimes you don't even realize you're doing it, as this next story reveals.

In HGTV's first year, the founding team decided to go off-site and have a retreat in Atlanta. There were many issues around strategy and growth that needed vetting, so we hired a moderator to move us through the two-day meeting. There were six men in the room and two women, me and the moderator. As she walked into the room and began to organize the day, it was clear the guys were distracted by something. There were quiet side jokes I couldn't quite hear. Then, I looked more closely at her. Her blouse was sheer and flimsy and clung to her upper assets. Which appeared to be . . . well, cold.

I spoke to her on our first break and she grabbed a blazer to wear for the rest of the meeting. But like my backward skirt, the trip wire had been hit. No man has to worry if it's cold in the room and his form-fitting shirt shows it. Women, on the other hand, do.

I once read about a female Harvard professor who was so concerned about a wardrobe malfunction during lectures that she always wore suits when she taught, and her tops underneath were invisibly secured to her skin with double-sided tape. Seemed like a lot of work, and pretty uncomfortable to me. But I understand where she's coming from.

There's also the unwelcome matter of being seen *and* heard walking into a room. Do you announce your presence at a meeting with an arm party of bracelets and bangles?

In the beginning of my career I made many mistakes with dress until I learned the best style for me, which was essentially a neutral, classic, but still feminine look with soft, pretty blouses or dresses accompanied by a blazer or stylish sweater. I came to learn that owning nice blazers in various colors (except tangerine) was a lifesaver in making wardrobe choices easier.

Another aspect of good work dress is the importance of the final touches. If your shoes are scuffed or your fingernails chewed and torn, they will detract from an otherwise polished look.

Getting the right spit and polish—finishing touches—on wardrobe is worth the investment. It signals you belong on the best team on the field.

Like it or not, every day, what you're wearing gets a once-over. What I would term power-neutral is safest, not much flash but a classic look with good spit and polish. A classic look is understated, fresh, sleek, and appears high-end. (Look to buy clothing as a fashion season ends, for the next year. Great bargains!) Even then, don't be surprised if someone makes a comment. In *Tough Choices*, Carly Fiorina recounted an interview with *Business Week* her first week on the job as CEO of Hewlett-Packard. One of the first questions she was asked: Was her suit Armani?

Business Casual

The peskiest wardrobe issue I've confronted is that dastardly "business casual." After thirty years in business, I still don't know what it means.

When business casual first made its way into the workplace, it seemed like such a good idea. But unfortunately, it has turned out to be a bit of a hornet's nest for everyone in business because nobody can really define it.

Here's what Ann Drake, CEO of DSC Logistics, has to say on the topic:

> *Years ago I figured out that the words were different and the results were different for women versus men. For example, if a woman wears a tucked-in logo shirt like a man will wear, the woman looks less dressed up than the man. So here's what I've counseled our women. I tell them if we have a business casual day, you can wear a nice logo shirt but add a jacket. So business casual in our company usually means that for the women, it includes a blazer. And if the men are supposed to wear a jacket for an event, the women usually wear a pantsuit it or a skirt suit.*

Women need to dress a notch above men in a business casual setting. Short-sleeved shirts are acceptable on men, for example, but can make women look underdressed. Again, a working woman's best investment is a blazer. They can dress up your business casual look in a hurry. You can always take them off when you're sitting in the meeting. Just throw it back on during the breaks and when you depart.

If you are too casual, it can signal disrespect for the workplace or any other institution. You may recall the ruckus around some girls on Northwestern University's championship lacrosse team wearing flip-flops to the White House in 2005. The news tore through the media with an outcry of how disrespectful that was to the White House. The workplace is the same way. If you dress too casually you may signal to the veteran players that you're not taking this game called business seriously enough. Why risk it?

Special Occasions

What happens when you need to trade in your regular work attire for a special occasion? There are uniform requirements for those events too. Let's look at some common ones.

Black-Tie Dinners

At a black-tie event, that little black dress can be worn well or can set you back in your professional life. You can trip up by wearing your LBD so tightly you have to descend a stairway sideways to move in it. Moreover, a little black dress cut too low or with the hemline too high can also send the wrong message. I know I sound like a wet blanket on this topic. It's a party, right? But really, it's not. It's still work, and the people around you are still your work colleagues, many of whom are men.

Halloween

Many workplaces hold Halloween parties, and this is another situation where caution in dress must prevail. I once saw a female colleague come in as Catwoman. She was proud of looking good in that costume, and I would be too if I had her physique *and* it was a non-work event. She genuinely hadn't considered the message such a form-fitting costume could convey.

Rule of thumb: At work Halloween parties, your costume can be silly but not sexy.

Good Luck Garments

Many athletes have superstitions, rituals they repeatedly do either before or during a game that they believe are good luck and propel them to top performance. It could be always lacing up the right cleat before the left, or a certain handshake with a fellow player before a big game. Some wear certain jewelry, like a medal or cross because without it they'd risk poor performance.

I too had certain clothing I'd wear when I needed to be on top of my game. During the biggest deal negotiations I'd wear my diamond earrings. During speeches I'd wear my Mikimoto diamond-studded pearl necklace. Still do. These are my power pieces; they always made me feel in control enough to win in high-stakes situations.

WHY UNIFORMS ARE ACTUALLY GOOD

I've spent a lot of this chapter trying to communicate how you can avoid disaster in your dress—don't be sexy or flashy or too casual. There are a lot of don'ts. But I'll close by saying that I think dress codes are helpful. First off, they simplify our choices. Moreover, when you wear the uniform, you send out the message that you want playing time. You're telling everyone that you are serious, that you respect your company and yourself enough to take the time to dress like a professional. When you suit up, you remind them: I'm here, and I'm here to win.

YOUR TURN

1. If you like feminine garments, wear them. Just be sure your tops aren't so sheer that undergarments can be seen. Good habits include wearing a camisole and, when needed, a blazer.

2. Avoid wearing clothing cut too low or too tight or with hemlines too high in any work situation. You have a little more leeway at black-tie events, but not a lot.

3. Dry-cleaners are your friend. Budget some money for dry-cleaning and tailoring when you buy wardrobe items.

4. Purchasing cotton blends and wrinkle-resistant fabrics will be time-savers as you're getting dressed in the morning because they usually don't require pressing.

5. Men and women are held to different definitions of business casual; women must meet a higher standard. Bring along a blazer or nice sweater to notch up the professionalism of your look.

6. A worthwhile addition to any bedroom or door area is a full-length mirror. A quick look before you head off to work is a good insurance policy against wardrobe malfunctions. Like skirts on backward.

7. Shoes can be worn with color to brighten an outfit, but make sure they're not scuffed up and in disrepair. Boots are fine and can be a nice accessory. Heels are a personal choice and depend a lot on your height and that of the men you deal with.

8. Wearing too much jewelry can look gaudy. You want a simple, elegant look. And make sure your jewelry is always on mute!

9. Like heels, makeup is a very personal situation. I know women who wear no makeup and look beautiful. I know women who wear it all the time and look beautiful. There's no right answer to this question.

PART
TWO

The first seven chapters focused on building a panoply of skills to be a proficient, competitive, winning executive. The remaining chapters deal with having strong reserves of emotional maturity. Emotional maturity rounds out the complement of skills you bring to the corner office.

In the workplace you will see evidence of emotional maturity in three key ways: the sportsmanlike way you handle wins and losses, the grit you possess to push through difficult times, and the ways you express yourself in team dynamics. These will be explored in the remaining three chapters.

When you get these right, you'll have reached a profound level of emotional maturity. You will have arrived as a leader.

Chapter 8

Exhibit Good Sportsmanship

RULE 8: GOOD SPORTSMANSHIP

The Game Context: Players should be gracious, in victory or defeat. Everyone loves a good sport; everyone hates a sore loser—or worse, a smug winner.

The Business Setting: Grace attracts others to want to work with you—colleagues, staff, and management. Practicing good sportsmanship builds emotional maturity and mental toughness, which then builds you into a leader.

THE PERFECT GAME. ALMOST.

This true story stars three people: a pro pitcher, his manager, and an umpire. In the summer of 2010, a twenty-eight-year-old, unspectacular pitcher for the Detroit Tigers named Armando Galarraga found himself one out away from a perfect game. A perfect game is the absolute finest game a pro pitcher can deliver. Only twenty-one pitchers in the long history of America's pastime had ever done it. He was one out away from being vaulted into the baseball elite.

With two out in the ninth, Armando delivered a pitch. The batter got a piece of it and began running to first. When he got there the ball had been fielded and thrown to first. Man out! *Except*, first-base umpire Jim Joyce called the runner safe.

Everyone could see it was the wrong call. The stands erupted. Tigers manager Jim Leyland came running out of the dugout. Chaos ensued.

But what was done was done. To preserve the legacy of the game at that time, there was no call review in baseball except for homerun challenges, and no instant replays, like in other pro sports. Armando's perfect game was lost.

Later that night umpire Jim Joyce watched the tape and saw he'd blown the call, costing this pitcher a chance at national fame and likely fortune. Meanwhile, Armando kept quiet. No badmouthing Jim. No complaints.

The following night, at Comerica Park in downtown Detroit, 28,000 fans booed and hissed Jim Joyce when they saw him on the field again, getting ready to ump the game. Suddenly the whole place went quiet. Armando emerged from the dugout, holding something.

He made a slow walk to Jim. Armando handed Jim the lineup card for the night and shook his hand.

Jim Joyce broke down and cried on national television. He later issued a formal apology to Armando for his grave mistake. When asked about that by reporters, this remarkable pitcher had three simple words: "Everyone makes mistakes."

So Armando Galarraga did not go down in baseball history for pitching a perfect game. Instead, he'll be remembered as a courageous, unspectacular pitcher who refused to play the victim. He's a shining example of good sportsmanship at its finest.

WHY BE A GOOD SPORT?

If business is really about winning, why be a good sport?

The fact is, whether you win or lose, good sportsmanship matters. It matters as part of our societal framework, part of our culture, and it reinforces treating others with respect and dignity. Think of an NFL game and what happens at the end, before the network cuts back to the studio. The camera follows the postgame ritual of handshakes. The coaches come out and shake hands. All the team players approach one another on the field and go through the good sportsman ritual: good game, nice game, congratulations.

That's part of the televised game because it matters to us to see our professional athletes do that. And when they don't—when a player skulks off to the locker room in a huff, when a coach refuses to shake his or her counterpart's hand—that's news. That's bad behavior. And we as a culture criticize it as such.

Tennis player John McEnroe was known for his center court temper tantrums. He threw his racquet. He berated line judges. He yelled and held up game play with his antics. He dominated postgame press conferences with his bellyaching. Meanwhile, Martina Navratilova was all business on the court. No yelling, bickering, or tantrum throwing. She was an aggressive competitor on the court who was also known for her off-court friendship with rival Chris Evert. The two met on the court eighty times. And often they would travel together to the next tournament. They developed a respectful friendship. Fans gravitated to them as role models. They liked them. Many tolerated John McEnroe only because they wanted to see some good tennis.

Consider these three tennis greats. Then ask yourself:

* Who would you rather work for?
* Who would you hire?
* Who looks like someone you'd want to do business with?
* Which one would you want on your work team?

This value of good sportsmanship extends from the field into all kinds of contests, and naturally that includes business, since business is a grand contest. There are winners and losers. It's a constant cycle of competition. When we display good sportsmanship, we see positive results. When we don't, our reputations suffer.

And yet, it's an element many women fail to develop to their advantage.

DEVELOPING THE GOOD
SPORTSMAN ADVANTAGE

Back in the chapter on practice, I said that it takes more than knowledge to be good at something. It takes more than skill. We all know that it takes practice.

Well, by the time men and women arrive in the business world, men have had a lot more practice than women in the art of good sportsmanship.

This is true even today as sports have opened up for girls, and opportunities for them to play at a higher level have exploded. While boys and girls may both play sports, boys are constantly in competition—whether it's "Race you to the corner" or "Last one in is a rotten egg" or "Shotgun!" Boys compete all the time, in just about everything, so really, much of their lives is an exercise in good (or bad) sportsmanship.

I was a girl of the era when sports were for boys. I went to college at a time when men played and women (mostly) cheered. And yet I have made it a career practice to be a good sport because it works.

How Good Sports Turn Lemons into Lemonade

Most of us have been turned down for a promotion at least once. There are two ways to handle this type of situation:

By acting professionally
By being a victim

The latter has a distinctive sound to it. It includes phrases like *it's unfair* (and it may be), *they just don't like me* (and they might not), or *I was more deserving* (and you likely were). None of that matters. The most important thing is to hold your head high and to learn from it. Why did that other person get the job? What dynamics were at play in the final analysis? Ask the decision makers, but not with bitterness. Ask only as a lesson you can chalk away for next time. That's the hallmark of a good sport.

I lost a job to run the national affiliate sales team for CNBC as its senior vice president. When those of us on the ground floor were beginning CNBC, we had several CEOs. NBC finally landed on Roger Ailes, currently CEO of Fox News Channel and former Republican political strategist. Roger was a larger-than-life presence who seemed to know everyone who was anyone. He had a certain carriage about him that made one pay attention. He chose his allies carefully, and it seemed I was one, as I came from the affiliate sales world where he had no connections or prior experience. When I came to the corporate headquarters from my regional Detroit office on business, I'd stop by his office, and he usually had time for me.

The senior vice president job came open, and I applied. I was up against David Zaslav, who was a promising young lawyer at the time, housed at headquarters in Fort Lee. (In Chapter 5, I wrote of the trust David and I had built up.)

I recall the morning the call came through. Linda, our Detroit receptionist, came running into my office out of breath, announcing, "It's Roger Ailes on the line!" Because Roger wasn't one to call into the Detroit office with any regularity (as in, never), she was abuzz.

I thought, *Well, here we go*, and picked up the line. Roger quickly got to the point. "I chose David, Susan. He's here, he knows the place, he knows the business, and he's a lawyer. You do good deals, but you're not a lawyer."

I couldn't argue the point, and I had no plans to run out and get a law degree.

Somehow I found the wherewithal to elevate my good sportsmanship to a new level. I called David and congratulated him. No hard feelings. I gave him the proverbial handshake over the phone.

I realized after Roger called that my advancement at NBC was limited. I had no plans to spend three years in law school if that's what mattered to management. Fortuitously, two months after I was turned down for that job, the HGTV job was offered, and I accepted. On my last day, David called to wish me good luck and said we must stay in touch. And we have.

Good sportsmanship tactics include:

- Asking for and receiving management's feedback regarding why you were not chosen, so you can learn from it.
- Remaining professional and reaching out to the winner, acknowledging his or her win.
- Coming to work the next day not showing any of your ego bruises from the loss.
- Strategizing what advancement looks like for you, given these experiences.

I'm hardly the only person to realize that being a good sport in a disappointing situation can pay dividends down the road. Colleen Repplier is president of Tyco Fire Protection Products, a global $1.6 billion strategic business unit within Tyco. Colleen was all set to move into a brand-new senior position in her company before she joined Tyco, when the world shifted beneath her:

> *The plan was that I would be moved into a role to become head of a new unit that my CEO was creating, and I had actually already found my replacement and effectively backfilled my former position. I was to run a new business segment that would comprise a portfolio of acquisitions focused in a new direction and in a growth area for the company. But then there was a spin-off and our unit was sold to private equity. And the new owners said they were not spending cash buying any more companies, so that strategy for the promised new job wasn't going forward.*

At first, Colleen's boss tried to save her promotion and told her she could run one of the other business units in the new company. It seemed like a good fit. But, Colleen explained, "There was already a leader in place there, and he'd been president of that division for many years. My CEO wanted to remove that person and to put me into that role, so he went to the equity partners' board and said he wanted to make the change, put me in charge. And the board said no. Too risky; they wanted to keep the existing leaders in those roles, as they have a lot of contacts and relationships."

So now, Colleen had no promotion to move into and no actual job to stay in. Yet she was contractually obligated to this company.

> *I was locked into the company both emotionally and financially, with no real job. I was locked in with the normal hooks that most buyers put in place when purchasing a company, in order to maintain the continuity of the leadership team through a time period beyond the sale.*

Soon after the disappointment came the opportunity: the chance to run the fire products business for Tyco. And Colleen was able to capitalize on the gracious way she'd handled herself during the merger chaos. "I had a good relationship with my CEO," she said. "So I told him about the offer, and how I was ready to run a larger business, and he acknowledged he didn't have that for me where I was. So he went to bat for me and got the board to release the financial and contractual constraints."

She reflected on how she had handled this like any good sport would:

> I think had I been overly emotional about that loss, it wouldn't have been such a good outcome because it would have created friction and alienated me from my CEO and the new owners of the company. Sometimes you just have to accept you're not going to get everything you want, you're not always going to win. So when you lose, you've got to just step back and say, OK, let's move on to Plan B.

Good sportsmanship is not just a personal strategy. It can be deployed for the good of a team. Ann Drake tells the story of losing a big client and how she kept her head in the long-term game through practicing good sportsmanship:

> We had a good customer and, slowly, over five years, we lost the existing business and any new business to all of our competition. Sometime later, one of our guys got a call saying there was a new bid coming up and this former customer wanted us to bid on it. He came into my office and said, "What should we do?"
>
> I thought we should go for it. And I remember having a hard time getting the team real interested, but we did it, and we lost it.

So I said, "We've got to understand what happened here." We asked
two people from the client's customer team to come to our corporate
office and give us a debrief, which they did.

And I remember thinking, boy, they're being pretty forthright
just coming to talk with us. Usually you won't get an answer as to
why you lost a bid. Then, two months later, this company asked us
to bid again. I called the team together and said, "What do you
want to do?" And the main guys who had to do the bid work said,
"Well, OK, it won't be a lot of work." So we made the bid and we
won. And we've been winning ever since. They are now an absolutely
major customer of ours again. It took five years to lose them, but
we kept coming back and over the last three to four years we got the
business back.

By remaining professional and engaged, Ann's team won that
client back.

Winning and Good Sportsmanship

When I was at HBO, I moved four times in eight years. Two of those
times were for promotions, and I beat out someone who resided in
that office. It was a double whammy for them because by all rights
they should have had the inside track, given they knew the office
workings and the clients. The first time this happened I dealt with
it when I first arrived, walking into the guy's office and closing the
door to talk with him. He was a genuinely nice man, not a jerk, so I
felt bad for him. But that's the thing about sales. The numbers don't
lie. He and I talked, and I learned they were giving him a smaller
territory, but keeping him, so he seemed OK about things. By ac-

knowledging my win in a nonthreatening, nonboastful way, I practiced good sportsmanship.

The next situation was harder, because the gentleman I beat out would now report to me. When I arrived, I met the whole team, and afterward I made a beeline to his office and we talked. I expressed my interest in having him remain on my team. He too was a good guy. (I was lucky in these instances!) When I first started work there, I made sure the rest of the team knew I valued his contributions. I figured if this had happened to me I'd want the same respect paid.

Being a good sport in a win means being gracious and proactive toward the losing party, even if he's acting like a sore loser. You don't want him sabotaging you, so the best thing you can do is to go into his office, close the door, and acknowledge that the promotion went to you but that will be old news tomorrow, and you hope that the two of you can still work together comfortably. It may not work, but you've made the effort. In the end you can only control your own behavior, and your reputation.

WOMEN, GOOD SPORTSMANSHIP, AND THE BIG PICTURE

In every competition, there is a winner and there is a loser. Even in a solitary game like golf, a good golfer is competing to beat others or their handicap, or to break par. It can be unsettling to realize that business is one grand competition, and there are always winners and losers. One party gets the better deal, the better job, the promotion you wanted, the better office. Good corporate cultures will try to keep their workplace harmonious, but the winners and losers always emerge.

Success is when you can count more wins than losses in some span of time, say a day, a week, or a month. You will never get *all* the wins because that's grossly unrealistic. From the standpoint of emotional maturity, success is coping with your losses and objectively learning from them, being a good sport about them. Boys who play team sports have had so much practice with losses (as well as wins) growing up that most appear to take loss in stride in the workplace. They have learned how to keep a cool head because they know losing is not the end of the world.

Women might understand that beating a client for the best deal means the company wins, so we're good with that. But beating out a colleague is uncomfortable because we are raised to be nice, cooperative ladies. We need to get over ourselves. While you're fretting about these nonissues, the guys are back in their offices devising the next strategy to beat you.

Most of us don't get the win on the first try. Good gamers regroup and ramp up for the next competitive situation. U.S. endurance swimmer Diana Nyad walked ashore on September 2, 2013, to become the first person to swim from Cuba to Florida. This was her fifth try. She was sixty-four years old.

Emotional reactions to losing, like embarrassment, shame, or fear, will perpetuate more losses in the workplace because you'll look vulnerable, exposed. You need to keep your cool even if you have a bundle of stomach-churning nerves. Gamers overcome emotions like fear and defeat and appear undaunted, unruffled. They may not feel that way, but they don emotional armor to go onto the field to compete again. Operating from shame or fear makes your body tense, and that strain upsets your rhythm. Like the pro pitcher who puts his foot back on the rubber after he just walked the last batter, it's a fresh new start every morning you come to work.

YOUR TURN

1. Always seek out management to learn why you didn't get an assignment or promotion. Ask with dispassion and a sincere desire to learn from the loss. You may not get the whole truth, but taking this action shows management you're still mentally in the game. And you want the next win.

2. Being a good sport means being emotionally mature enough to show professionalism at work, in good times and in the tough ones. Emotional maturity is a key component of leadership.

3. Maintain relationships with your colleagues and clients after you experience a work loss to them. Holding your head high, showing professionalism, opens you up to future wins from them.

4. If you're the victor in the game, always be gracious to the loser. This protects your reputation, and oh, by the way, it's the right thing to do.

5. Don't ever apologize or feel sheepish about your wins. Management chose you because they believed you were the better candidate for the job.

6. Don't forget that losses can open new doors if you act with grace and fortitude and are willing to extract the lessons they teach.

Chapter 9

Show True Grit

The Game Context: When difficulties occur, gamers with grit become even fiercer competitors. If they get hurt, they learn to quickly dismiss a scraped knee, but they pay close attention to internal bleeding and find ways to fix it. They step up when the game is really on the line.

The Business Setting: Grit is mental toughness. It is the warrior within you that enables your career advancement even when there are setbacks. It's your ability to find the inner strength to push ahead and stay in the game as well as the outer stamina that keeps you moving forward.

GRIT: THE FUEL FOR STAMINA AND GROWTH

At the 1996 Olympic Games in Atlanta, Kerri Strug was a member of the U.S. women's gymnastics team, tagged by the media as the Magnificent Seven. Going into the final rotation of the team competition, the U.S. women were leading the Russians. Then one of the members of the U.S. team, Dominique Moceanu, fell twice on her vault, registering a poor score. Kerri was the last to vault.

Kerri underrotated her first vault, turning her ankle on the landing. She needed a clean second vault for the United States to take the gold. As she approached the runway for her second vault, she was limping. She landed the second vault briefly on both feet, then hopped to her good foot to salute the judges. She then collapsed to her knees and needed help off the landing platform. Sportscaster John Tesh covering the event commented, "Kerri Strug is hurt! She is hurt badly."

The U.S. Team won the gold. Kerri Strug, with a sprain and tendon damage that would keep her out of the rest of the Olympic competition, was carried to the podium in the arms of her coach, Béla Károlyi. Kerri was an instant celebrity—lauded in the media for her skill, her dedication to her team, and her spectacular display of grit.

Where does this kind of grit come from? That fierce competitive drive that propels someone, against all odds, to win when the game's really on the line?

Grit is really a multifaceted state, and I'll look at it here in three ways: I'll first look at grit as a manifestation of *resilience*—the ability to bounce back from disappointment, to not be weighed down by temporary hurdles, and to find the energy necessary to handle the daily challenges of life. Second, I'll look at grit as a *defensive weapon*— a way to strike back when life hits you the hardest. This kind of grit is not everyday resilience but the inner strength you need when the really bad stuff happens. And finally, I'll look at grit as *courage*. We are all afraid of things. It is normal, natural, and even healthy sometimes to experience fear. But when fear gets in your way, you need to face it and defeat it. That too takes a particular type of grit.

GRIT AS RESILIENCE

It's simple. Will beats skill every time. Baseline talent gets you into the game. Winning, however, takes staying power. Professional athletes fascinate me, yes because they are great physical specimens, but mostly because their drive is unrelenting, much like Kerri Strug's. Michael Jordan hit under 50 percent of his shots for points, yet he is considered by many the greatest player in basketball. The best guys at the plate have batting averages under .400, meaning that they make outs more than half the time. In professional athletics it's all about the numbers, and the players know they will succeed less than half the time. But they keep at it, with grit and determination. They understand that loss is just a part of gamesmanship, that it spurs you on to step up your game and to press for the next win. Repetition with loss—of all kinds—teaches you that you can, indeed, bounce back from disappointments, and if you're willing to practice the next time, you just might win. Resilience is about pushing through loss, learning from it, and keeping the faith that next time will be better. Just keep pressing ahead and practicing, and the next time you'll win.

In the toughest of times you learn the value of having grit. Learning from losses makes you stronger. Some call it the healing power of heartbreak. Heartbreak and defeat unlock your inner reserves of strength. To suffer defeat is no less a part of living than to experience joy or love. It is from these all-too-human experiences that we pull grit from our very soul. We become the victor, not the victim. There is redemption. Defeat becomes a springboard to lead a deeper, richer life.

It's ironic that many women view themselves as inadequate when handling situations requiring resilience. Yet day after day, you call it up with the many roles you juggle—worker, caregiver, home organizer, school volunteer—and the myriad challenges each of these poses.

I embraced the queen chess piece for the book cover for a reason. The queen is the most powerful chess piece on the board. Like the queen, with its ability to move in any direction on the chessboard, so too are you able to bounce from one challenge to the next, putting fires out with your inner strength and resilience. Many associate tough grit with men. In my experience it's women who are really gifted with great reserves of grit.

The quality of resilience is one of the great puzzles of human nature, and while the research is still in its infancy, scientists are beginning to make sense of it through predictive tools. Angela Duckworth, a psychologist at the University of Pennsylvania, made the study of resilience part of her life's work. In the article "The Truth About Grit" by Jonah Lehrer, she described tools to predict success. Two factors, perseverance and conscientiousness, are more predictive of success than intelligence. In other words, grit can trump brains. Single-minded pursuit is often a factor in great success, she found.

From her work, Angela concluded that the better job applicants are those who have pursued one certain hobby for years, rather than a renaissance type of individual who may have pursued many hobbies. This may explain why companies like General Electric screen applicants for those who have played a college sport of some sort. Playing sports at a college level takes talent but it also takes a healthy supply of grit—an ability to pursue excellence even when new people, exciting new experiences, and new freedom may beckon. Oh, and there's also that little matter called *going to class*. It takes determination and discipline—grit—to be a good athletic and academic college player.

Diane Coutu, a senior editor at *Harvard Business Review*, came up with another way to look at grit through the filter of how organizations function. She synthesized existing research on resilience and came up with three factors that made organizations more resilient than others:

- An acceptance of reality
- Deep beliefs in larger value systems
- Remarkable ability to improvise

Let's look more closely at these three factors.

Accepting Reality

Those people who are willing to face losses with a mature sense of reality help businesses withstand tough times. This means they learn to not personalize tough things that may happen at work. Perhaps it takes many birthdays to realize this, but most of what evolves in organizations has nothing to do with us. We're in the audience, not on the stage. Even being fired may have nothing to do with us during group layoffs. Accepting reality is about learning to have a more detached and mature perspective.

Value Systems

Resilient people are those who believe that their job mission is a part of a larger picture or more meaningful future. This could come from the belief in the larger mission or culture of the organization or from beliefs outside the workplace. They are much like video gamers who embrace the epic meaning in the games they play. Sure, it's a game. But to the dedicated gamer, it's about battling the bad guys and making sure good triumphs over evil.

When people visited the HGTV building as we were growing, our visitors would describe our employees as happy, helpful, and energized. Our wise adviser Dr. Steve Martin explained that home represented sanctuary and safety to most people. It represented belonging. Our home-based mission was rooted in what our employees could connect with and hold dear. They bought into it, indeed, lived it because their work mission lined up well with their values of home.

Sometimes negative things happen at work. When you face these with a view that it is just part of a larger, unfolding plan, you eschew self-pity. It's helpful to think, This happened for a reason; I may not see that right now, but I know it will help when I'm in this situation again. If I hadn't experienced this, what things wouldn't I have otherwise learned? For example, losing a job at CNBC was tough emotionally, but I learned a critical nugget of truth. At NBC a law degree was highly valued for sales advancement, at least for that moment in time while I worked there. I had no desire to run out and get one, so my advancement was limited there. This allowed me to leave the place with an objective, non-emotional point of view. And it taught me to ask the next time around if specialized experience was important for salespeople.

Ability to Improvise

You find the ability to improvise in many successful startup organizations and in the entrepreneurial people there who zig and zag, often morphing their business models as they grow. In established organizations, you find it where real empowerment occurs at the operational level. In other words, the corporate office has a realistic view of what it knows, and what it doesn't know, what it should do and not do, and allows its people the freedom to win within large, agile operating parameters.

Having to find ways to solve problems without the resources at HQ makes for scrappy, resilient employees. Some of the grittiest people I have worked with were housed in regional offices, where they had to make decisions and act quickly without the benefit of corporate resources around them. Salespeople are typically in these offices, and it takes a lot of grit to be in sales. Sales folks hear no—a loss—so often, then face the next day with new reserves of grit to get a yes the next time around.

One gritty salesperson who comes to mind is Ruth Tatom, who ran SNI's Los Angeles office for many years. On 9/11, she was in New York and five months pregnant with her first child. She was a high-risk pregnancy and 2,800 miles away from her doctors and her home. When I first spoke with her in New York, her voice quivered but she said she was sure she would, somehow, find her way home soon. I hated that she was in such a tough bind. With all air and rail transportation canceled and no rental cars available anywhere, it would be difficult. She had tried all those means and kept pressing on to get home. Yet, much like a video gamer exhibits urgent optimism and doesn't let challenges get in the way, a few days later Ruth had solved her conundrum. She was in a van with other people from Los Angeles, whom she had managed to locate and connect with in New York. They were driving cross-country. Three months later she delivered a healthy little girl named Elsa.

Grit does not come to us easily. Often we need to dig for it—or take the advice of a mentor to make that happen. Meredith Vieira, a former ABC News correspondent, shared a story at a conference I attended about rebounding from the shame of being fired. She was early in her career, and her boss called her in on a Friday. (Note: Beware of unscheduled Friday meetings with your boss. This is a very popular day to get fired.) He said she didn't have what it takes to be successful, and she was fired. She went home and was crying in her room when her dad came in. He asked her what was wrong and she told him, with trepidation and embarrassment, that she was fired. She said her boss told her she didn't have what it takes. He paused, then asked: "What do *you* think?" She looked at her dad and said she didn't agree with her rotten boss. And then she got mad.

The following Monday she walked into her boss's office and told him she *did* have what it takes! And she told him *why*. Guess what? She was rehired.

These are good examples of grit—the resilience type—in action.

GRIT AS DEFENSE

There's another kind of grit—the kind you call on when life throws the really bad stuff at you. In dark times, you need a special kind of grit.

The Road Can Be Unsafe for a Woman

When I work with young women today, many seem to feel they are ten feet tall and invincible. I remember feeling that way too when I was just starting out, with all the promise of an exciting future ahead of me. I was naive regarding what could happen when traveling on business. What follows is a story that occurred early in my career, and until now the only people who have ever known of it are my husband and a sister who, a few years later, would also be a victim of this same violence. Much later I would talk to a counselor about it.

It was 1981, and I had been doing business travel for about a year. As I was entering my hotel room and fiddling with the key, a man across the hall was entering his. He smiled and I smiled back. That was it—until later that night. I had been out for dinner and drinks and was feeling no pain from the good wine I'd consumed as I entered my room. I had no sooner dropped my key on the desk than there was a knock on the door.

I saw through the keyhole it was the guy across the hall I'd seen that morning. I opened the door. Yes, I know now that was an incredibly stupid thing to do, but he had just seemed so sincere and earnest with that morning smile, and now looking at me through the keyhole. I guess I felt ten feet tall and invincible. When I began to open the door, he pushed in and it was clear he didn't need any hotel help, as I had imagined.

I asked him to leave, but that didn't happen. I began to feel the cold flood of fear. What followed is an ugly account of being assaulted. I realized how true it was that my physical strength would pose no resistance to a man. I had no weapons and no training to fight him off.

If you have ever been assaulted, I am so very sorry. You likely handled it better than I did. I didn't report it. I was in shock. I sat staring out the window until dawn and flew home. I didn't tell anyone. I didn't seek counseling. I know now that the best thing one can do is to get help, to be able to say the words and share what happened to a trained professional. I didn't do any of that. Who knows why; perhaps I felt shame, or just did not want to relive any of it again. Perhaps I was in denial, which can be a shock absorber for the psyche when things are just too hard to take in.

Or perhaps, at twenty-six years of age, I didn't understand that emotional pain is no different from physical pain. It too needs to be treated. Emotional pain needs emotional convalescence, just like physical injuries do. In the end, it's more courageous to ask for help than it is to press on without getting any.

While it might not have been the best of choices, what I did was rely on my inner grit to get me through. When you can move on and at least get back to the rhythm of old routines, you become a victor, not the victim.

On the Road:
Tips for the Female Traveler

1. Be sure to examine a whole hotel room when you enter, preferably while your bellman waits or does it with you. I've entered several hotel rooms where it was clear someone else already occupied it, which means we both had keys to the same room.

2. Always use deadbolts when inside your room.

3. Use your peephole to screen for any strangers before opening your door.

4. There are martial arts classes given by local police departments, nearby universities, and privately. Some methods include krav maga, jujitsu, and tae kwon do.

5. RAD stands for Rape Aggression Defense and is another method for self-defense. It's taught at many local colleges and universities.

Workplace Tragedies and Grit

Sometimes the life of a coworker unravels with such force that grit is called for just to get through the experience.

I had left HBO to join a turnaround company called Z Channel. This was a subscription channel that had been in Los Angeles a long time. It was Hollywood's darling, showing every kind of movie imaginable. The creative genius behind the network was a man named

Jerry Harvey. We met for breakfast at Stuckey's, a legendary Los Angeles haunt, when I was interviewing for the job. Jerry had wild red hair and wore a lighter hanging on a chain around his neck, which he used constantly as he chain-smoked. He talked in a mumble that was hard to make out, but I got enough of it. He was a walking encyclopedia of movie trivia with a passion for his movie-themed network. Somehow I passed his test and got hired. Jerry and I were to report to the owners.

Turnarounds can be messy and stressful, and we were a small team trying to make big decisions. At one point, we shifted strategies away from pure movies to include sports. Jerry was not happy about the new direction. But I would learn quickly that was just a tiny sliver of what was really going on with him.

In the middle of the strategy overhaul, on a warm Saturday afternoon, Jerry took out a gun and killed his wife, then himself.

I was married by then and my husband, Bill, was a great comfort. The next day, the team convened in the office. We all sat dumbfounded, in tears. We pulled everyone together, held hands around a small, beat-up conference table, and gave people a chance to say whatever was on their minds. We must have sat there for hours, just holding hands and airing whatever was bottled inside. Except me. I remember crying, but I said very little.

The memory of that Saturday afternoon stayed with me a long time. I thought of all the different ways this tragedy could have played out—involving me as victim—since I worked side by side with Jerry. I kept thinking, *There are lessons in all of this, but what are they?* After the services for him, we regrouped and pushed forward with more energy and commitment than before. Some did it in Jerry's memory; others, like me, who were angry and defiant pushed forward with an iron will, in spite of Jerry. Over the next year we tried many approaches, and eventually we sold Z's assets to Cablevision, who began another genre of network. Through it all, we relied on some deep reserves of grit and kept our forward momentum.

Emotional Pain Needs Time to Heal

We all have our 9/11 stories. I'm certain you have your own, and every one brings its own poignancy. I was traveling to New York that day and got as far as Atlanta, where the airport broke out in chaotic madness. There were some unsettling moments as we all wondered how far the scope of the attack would extend. In New York, we had over 200 employees in offices there, and some lost loved ones. With all of the gut-wrenching sadness that our employees were going through, plus my own pent-up despair, a little dam burst inside me. I finally recognized that the emotional pain I had buried and was carrying around was breaking my back. I needed help to get whole and to heal before I could find any peace to help others. I finally sought counseling for the rape, the Z Channel work violence, and the deep sadness I carried after 9/11.

It took me three tries, three separate encounters with tragedy to seek help, not just bottle it inside and ignore it. I learned that safety isn't just about whether you are lucky enough to live through a traumatic, life-changing event. It's about what happens afterward. And it's not just about the grit it takes to get through the event itself. It's about having the grit to also face the fallout, the toll that tragedies can take on the human psyche for a long time. I learned that there was a way to unload these burdens through sharing them with someone professionally trained who could receive and sort through them with me. By giving voice to these dark chapters in my life, I began learning how to free myself from the emotions attached to them. Healing comes when you can bring such darkness into the light. Going through this process, I found peace in seeing that these things hadn't been done to me, that I hadn't been singled out any more than other victims of violence are. Life just unfolds with all its light and its corresponding times of darkness. Being willing to seek help—that too is a process that calls for grit.

The events of 9/11 touched the heart and soul of our country and the whole world. The SNI story is ours, but there are thousands of other workplace stories of that day. Most workplace tragedies, however, have limited scope and impact to us. We read about them, feel badly for the company and those in harm's way, but they are seen through a distant lens. I realized this when I spoke with Amy Miles, CEO of Regal Entertainment. She recounted the fallout in her industry from the 2012 Aurora, Colorado, tragedy, in which a mass shooting occurred inside a theater multiplex during a midnight screening of the film *The Dark Knight Rises*:

When you hear about something that devastating, you immediately worry about the victims, but in this instance, since it hit so close to home having occurred in a movie theater, my mind quickly switched to our employees and customers. The first thing I thought of was, How can I help my employees feel safe? Our first priority was saying, Are we sure that our employees coming in today are safe? Some of our employees are sixteen years old. If they or their parents were not comfortable having them report into work, you schedule around it, and if it becomes an issue, go up the chain of command to figure out how to get help. You do not force that person to come in. And then, once we felt like our employees were safe, we examined our operations so we could be sure our customers would be protected and safe. Only after we made certain we had taken all possible measures to protect and care for our employees and customers was I personally able to absorb the extent of the tragedy.

All of life builds our grit. We build it layer by layer with each experience. There are transformational moments when you see the learning that comes from life experience. In the span of a moment, you feel changes happening *within* you. It's as if there is now an emotional blanket wrapped around your heart. It just doesn't hurt as much anymore. The holes there have become scars that you'll always carry with you, but they're no longer open wounds.

Sometimes we need others to help us with emotional healing and to build a durable, healthy kind of grit. Then, when the daily challenges of the workplace and life task us, we can draw on it.

GRIT AS EVERYDAY COURAGE

Courage is being scared to death, but saddling up anyway.
JOHN WAYNE

Earlier in this chapter I described women I meet who think they are invincible. The flip side of that are the women who have brains, spirit, and the desire to move forward in their careers, but are limited by fears. To be a great gamer, you need courage too. Courage is our last type of grit.

The word *courage* comes from the Latin root word for "heart." To succeed today, you need the heart of a winner. When you boldly break through fear instead of shuttering behind its walls, it's a liberating moment that can pay huge dividends in terms of both personal and career growth.

Fear can come from many sources: fear of failure, fear of work politics, or fear of appearing too grandiose in accomplishing things. You can have performance fear, which many athletes experience too but find a way to play through. It's human, indeed normal to have fears, and some fears keep us safe from harm. All of us have those moments where we're a bundle of stomach-churning nerves. Courage is acknowledging the fear and pushing through it.

I'm a fan of Shonda Rhimes, creator and producer of *Grey's Anatomy* and *Scandal*, because she creates such strong, fearless women in her shows. A journalist once asked her if it was good that women identify with these strong characters. Perhaps such strength is unrealistic. She responded that it's good to have strong and driven models who can help you to reach your goals. Shonda manages to create the right mix of characteristics in her female protagonists: They are human, but they don't seem fearful. She captures their inner strength and courage.

If only real life were that easy. In real life we fail a lot, but each failure teaches us something if we're open to being taught. We won't be perfect. The problem with fear is that it can find you wanting to stay in one place to avoid the discomfort of change. But in return for playing it safe in your well-defined world, you relinquish the sheer joy of personal and professional wins, which come only if you gamble a little on work and life. By standing still you're really moving backward, because others around you are pushing ahead. Fears can be very stifling and constrictive. They just make heavy going of life, and life is meant to be *enjoyed*, not just endured.

One of the reasons I love the gamer strategy is because it encourages you to begin to think of yourself as a winner, even though you will chalk up some losses. If you pay attention, you see that everyone experiences some losses along with their wins. When your career is viewed as a gamesmanship strategy, timidity and tentative views of your workplace fall away. Fears begin to dissolve. You practice winning and with enough practice, *you become a winner.* It's self-fulfilling.

The following are fear-based questions I've heard when working with aspiring career women, along with some answers. All these situations call for thought, action, and grit.

> Q: I don't know if I'm smart enough to run a company. I'm often derailed by my own doubts. How do I overcome this?
>
> A: I've wondered about that myself. How can I manage the numbers part of business, for example? What I learned is that, like anything else, it's just about practice. You find that it's fear, not lack of ability, that holds you back. The average Joe or Joan CEO is not some Mensa member. She's a person with some baseline ability who was willing to just keep at a skill until she's mastered it; then she moves on to the next one. It's all in the willingness to practice.
>
> You don't want to look back on your career twenty or thirty years from now and wish you had tried for the corner office. Just keep practicing. Then, like anyone who plays sports, you make muscle memory and create a new skill. Repetitions of practice will move you from adequate, to good, to great.
>
> Q: I've been working in an ad agency on the creative side. I like it, but I want to get into management. I'm afraid I don't have those left brain math and analytic abilities to do that job. What should I do?

A: How do you know you don't have some strong left brain skills until you try? Work on the courage to branch out and attempt something new.

Sharon John, president and CEO of Build-A-Bear Workshop, started on the creative side. She said in an interview that you can't use your natural gifts as an excuse to not master your development areas. She went on to get an MBA so she could more fully develop. That's one suggestion, but there are plenty of others in this book. It's all about being brave enough to practice new skills.

Q: I'm good with traveling in the United States, but I'm afraid to go overseas. Will that hold me down?

A: If you want to run a large corporation, it will definitely hold you down. If your aspirations are to run a smaller company then perhaps not, but it's hard to imagine any company today not selling goods overseas or sourcing materials and labor from there.

If your aspirations are not to run a company but to be a level or two down in the organization, then it might work for you. I can only say that overseas travel for me has been so broadening and has taught me life skills, like tolerance and understanding.

Q: My boss was fired. I'm terrified I'll lose my job now. How do I keep it?

A: As soon as is practical, make an appointment with your boss's boss. Ask her (or him) what her expectations for you are now that your boss is gone, and assure her you can live up to them. Set goals with her.

The cold truth is this, however. You may be on the chopping block as part of a larger reorganization or downsizing. *You* are not always responsible for being let go. In that case your Plan B is to role-play how to explain your departure to a new employer and to begin looking as soon as possible.

Q: I'd like to go back to school to get an MBA but I'm afraid I can't do the schoolwork and my job successfully at the same time. Any advice?

A: If you worked for me I'd discuss how we could make both work for you and for the company. You may need to cut back work hours, for example. Can you do that financially? Can I, as your boss, find others to step up while you're in school, or are those who you would recommend? In one of my management jobs I used what I called "borrowed executives." They came from other areas and wanted to pitch in for the chance to learn a new area. They cleared it with their supervisors and had to be able to handle both their primary job and the new assignment. It's short term and good learning for them and helps someone like you to pursue her dreams. But just to be clear: If I had any concerns about your duties not getting done, I'd ask you to wait until we could find the internal resources to support your move and manage what you're giving up.

Q: I see people around me getting chosen for task forces and training programs. Why aren't I on any of these lists?

A: Have you asked to be?

Q: I'm the only senior woman, and male colleagues hate me. I'm thinking of switching companies. What would you do?

A: The outcome of this situation fully rests with you, and the initiative you're willing to take. It's not up to your colleagues. Have you tried to build trust? Have you enlisted any of them for assistance or counsel on work you're doing? Have you graciously tried to support them in their endeavors? If you have done these things and you're still being shut out, then I'd switch companies too. Without cooperative colleagues or a cooperative culture, you won't be able to spread your wings and develop there. Sometimes, instead of looking for the grit to endure, what you really need is the grit to cut your losses and move on.

Please remember this: If we let our fears control us, we choose to play small. When we break through fears, we choose to play big.

YOUR TURN

1. When things get tough at work, remember that will beats skill. You've been put into your job because others believed you can do the work. You'll make mistakes; we all do. Tap your inner grit to mentally restart your day or week.
2. You should always go for the win, but it's grossly unrealistic to think you'll always get it. Everyone loses some days.

3. Loss feels more familiar and acceptable once it's happened a few times. Practice handling it with a cool head and resilience like athletes do, as a bridge to new learning and increasing your skills.

4. When you experience a loss, always ask yourself, What did I learn that can help me the next time I'm in this situation? Taking a strategic view engages your brain and quiets your emotions.

5. Mentors can be good supporters in times of loss. Seek yours out to discuss what occurred. If you are a mentor, listen, and then provide direction to move your mentee from emotion to strategy for how she will win the next time.

6. It's better to unload your fears and internal scars with a professional than to bottle them up. This will allow for quicker healing, more peace, and better job performance.

7. Minimize your risk to avoid risky and dangerous situations through engaging situational awareness. Situational awareness means having the presence of mind to stay vigilant of circumstances that could pose a personal threat to your safety. Limit or refrain from alcohol on the road so you're operating with maximum situational awareness.

Chapter 10

Be a Team Player

RULE 10: TEAM PLAY

The Game Context: Team play is how you win games. You can't always be the one to shoot the ball. Success in a team sport requires every player to understand that it's not just about scoring but how the human dynamics of the team support each individual.

The Business Setting: For women on the rise in the corporate world, two sets of teams matter. We need to manage within our work team and within our home team. Managing the home team is the hidden secret to successful work–life balance.

TEAM CHEMISTRY

In this chapter I'll look at two key teams: the work team and the home team. Let's start with the work team.

Alice Schroeder tells this story:

In 2001, I was invited to become a managing director at Morgan Stanley, which I gratefully accepted. Shortly thereafter, we held an orientation for the new managing directors in an auditorium, where a group of older former managing directors came on stage. They made a presentation about the firm and its values. One of them said, "I worked for Henry Morgan, who was the grandson of J. P. Morgan. You are the heirs of J. P. Morgan. I expect you to behave according to his principle that we will do first-class business in a first-class way. We will not take clients who are going to get us in trouble. We are not going to take risks that are going to get us in trouble." I was so proud to be a managing director that day. But by 2009, the firm had been through management turmoil, and many of the most talented people left and the culture of Morgan had eroded a lot.

How quickly a winning team can become a losing one. The success or failure of any team—and by extension any business—is due to its culture. This is a combination of its leadership, its values, and how the team gels to carry out its mission. In gamer terms it's called team chemistry. Watch any sport, and you'll see how each member of the team contributes his or her indispensable part to get the win. One great example is in football. One of the highest-paid positions is left offensive tackle. This guy guards his right-handed quarterback from blind-side hits. Offensive tackles garner large salaries because of this key role. The QB literally puts his health and career in the hands of this person. The trust is absolute. The chemistry is palpable.

The same goes in business. The culture of a place is based on its leadership, its values, and the trust each teammate has in one another. Over fifty years ago, renowned business management expert Peter Drucker began preaching that respect and trust in the corporate workplace increases results. Not all companies have caught on to this wisdom.

Good Team Chemistry, and Bad

Let's get the bad news out of the way first. Flawed cultures can still sometimes make for successful companies, at least in the short term. You may work at one of these. There is no trust among your teammates or management, but you have a unique, winning product or you have a bigger hammer, like more assets and cash, than your competition. I worked at a place like that. It was called NBC.

In the late 1980s, NBC decided it wanted in on the cable programming business. Its first foray was CNBC. I was on the ground floor of getting CNBC launched. We were a litigious culture that bullied its way to success. We used an asset we had and all other broadcasters had, called *retransmission consent*, to force cable operators into carrying us. Most other broadcasters used it as a carrot; we used it as the stick. While we bludgeoned our way into the business, our parent NBC was stingy with its one key asset—its powerful brand. We weren't allowed to put the eponymous peacock on any of our marketing materials. It seemed, from this junior executive's point of view, that they didn't trust us enough to build a winning business.

In essence we were only allowed to leverage the one thing our clients hated most, the hammer of retransmission consent. Customers had to sign these deals if they were to retain rights to carry NBC programming. I recall running into a client at a trade show who told me we were pigs and short-term players. I didn't trust management to have a winning, long-term view of the business, and they didn't trust us with their brand.

When a team has a flawed culture, it's tough to remain engaged, let along win for your company. Without mutual trust, it's hard for good employees to have staying power. You will invest in them, and they leave (thinking, Who *needs* this?) and you're left with the mediocre ones whom no one else wants. My longtime colleague Frank Gardner explains:

> *I've worked in some organizations that were totally dysfunctional, and they had been dysfunctional for years. We used to say, this place was built over an ancient burial ground. It's been screwed up for so long nobody could remember when it ever worked right. Nobody trusted anybody. The dysfunction was in the woodwork, in the paint, in the walls; it seeped into every pore of the place. Usually the people who survive in a place like that are the people who do very little, don't break anything further, just don't break any more dishes. That's a miserable place to be.*

From its first cable network, CNBC, NBC grew more cable network businesses. The next one was MSNBC. That channel was first called America's Talking, and I think its business plan was written on a napkin. There was no consumer proposition. It again was created out of the hammer of retransmission consent. Later, the NBC lawyers and deal makers forged a partnership with Microsoft and rebranded it MSNBC. It flailed for a long time with no ratings but eventually found a left-leaning brand voice and is profitable. Over time the small but valiant affiliate sales team, led by my friend Bridget Baker, pushed out more networks. NBC carriage continued to be an enormous trump card in getting deals done. Management began to see the wisdom of pulling the cable division into the fold once it began printing money for them.

When Frank and Ken recruited me for HGTV, we spent a lot of time discussing the importance of having great cultures—and terrible ones like those Frank described. We talked about the importance of trust. When we began to fill out the senior management team, many had come from broadcast companies with lots of infighting and politics, and we all wanted a fresh beginning without having to watch our backs.

Said Ken:

I was always of the opinion that whatever my work experience had been through life it was most successful when whatever place I was working for felt healthy, felt good. And it was usually because, first and foremost, there was trust. That took so much off your mind when you didn't have to sleep with one eye open at night.

A company's leadership creates and models the culture they're envisioning for their team and company. Good ones want a titanium-strength culture that will endure, a rock-solid foundation for building and sustaining their business. If you took a sample of Fortune 500 CEOs, many would tell you they spend a lot of time and energy on their company's values and culture. Ellen Kullman, chairman and CEO of DuPont, had been on a panel I'd moderated a few years back, and she'd told the crowd that brains alone won't get you a leadership role; you need a collection of critical skills. In follow up she explained to me that she looked for hybrid leaders, those who had the business acumen but who also knew how to motivate and bring their people along and develop them. In David Novak's organization, Yum! Brands, he has his management go through a three-day leadership development program called Taking People with You. It asks participants to rank themselves on truthfulness, openness, self-centeredness, and other personal attributes. The core nugget that cuts across good, healthy cultures is trust, which breeds good team chemistry.

It took me a while to learn and practice trust after my CNBC experience. One foolproof way to test what you're made of, especially in regard to trust, is when your team is about to expand through a company merger. And that's the subject of my next story.

Team Chemistry with New Players Coming Aboard

A successful client of mine once compared company turnarounds to baseball. He said it was all about hitting singles consistently instead of a few big home runs. Through a series of small and steady wins, you can turn around a company. When he said that, I thought back to 1997, when I was pushing for some big, booming home runs.

In the fall of 1997, E. W. Scripps, parent of HGTV, purchased the Food Network. HGTV headquarters were in Knoxville, Tennessee. The Food Network headquarters were in New York City. This proved to be a real mix of personalities and business styles. Food had been losing money; HGTV was on the brink of profitability in record time for a cable network. I had come to trust, unconditionally, my team at HGTV. But these new guys? Not so much.

It turned out to be an incredibly broadening experience for all of us who were hands-on with the merger. It employed most of my rules of gamesmanship to get it right, and I felt fortunate to be able to fall back on these rules as I was called on to help integrate two teams of people. Having said that, I stumbled along the way and applied the rules imperfectly.

We were firing on all cylinders with HGTV. I'm an impatient executive by nature, and I kept advocating to Ken that we decimate the senior team at Food so we could get our hands on it and, of course, fix it. He kept urging caution. In other words, let's hit singles and get some steady wins. As I mentioned earlier, Ken was always big on walking-around time, on getting to know people through sitting in a room or across the table with them. I was always big on *getting it done*, whatever *it* was. Ken's urging caution was the right approach. Let's look at why he was right, per the relevant gamer rules:

Rule 1: Conditioning. While, yes, HGTV staff had the requisite global, financial, and operational knowledge to run HGTV, how about a business based in the food capital of the country, New York City? We had no experience with New York unions, New York land leases, and local politics, just to name a few. We needed the institutional and technical knowledge of Food's senior team to broaden our own skill sets. Decimating them would have been a mistake.

Rule 2: Composure. Composure is about having poise even when you're not feeling it. I began to take deep breaths before I'd enter our joint meetings so I could slow myself down and really be present. I'll admit to continuing to want to move more quickly on structure changes than did Ken. One Sunday afternoon I was at the neighborhood pool with my son, and an HGTV salesperson called me with some news from a trade convention. One of Food's senior management had been on a panel preaching a strategy that would dig us further in the hole with our P&L. I marched into the pool house, called Ken, and unloaded. "We need to fire all of them!" I heard Ken sigh, again urge caution, and then tell me to just go take a jump in the pool to cool down.

Rule 6: Practice, practice, practice. Recall that in my definition, this means all things done before a game moment, this moment being winning new business, a coveted resource, or a promotion. These things include the important work of getting into the head of your colleague or competitor, which we do to better understand her job, as I did with climbing poles. When we practice, we can more readily project what's important to others and how they'll react to things. But first we have to take the time to do this practicing. Did I try to do that so we might best meld these teams? No, not really, or certainly not enough. Since we were the purchaser, these folks were likely scared to death for their jobs, and that may well have influenced their strained interactions with me. When I began to engage Rule 6, I came to learn how they saw the competitive playing field. I learned how they defined winning, from both a cultural standpoint and a financial standpoint.

Rule 8: Good sportsmanship. Because we were the acquirer, I had some hubris that clouded good judgment in evaluating the people we were inheriting. Remember, the one with the power must be the one with the grace. Purchasing and taking over a competitor was the biggest, coolest strategic win of my career, and for a short time I forgot to practice the rules. I felt like a rebel commander who'd just beaten the evil empire. I had to practice being a good sport and to see the new team as extra recruits who would help us win more games. They were no longer the competitors we'd cremated by acquiring them. I came to recognize that some of this team had incredible talent and was worth retaining when I began to practice Rule 8 with some emotional maturity.

Rule 9: Grit. I had impatient moments but came around to getting into their heads again. But how much grit does it take if you are on the receiving end of an acquisition? That's where one's grit is really tested because you are completely vulnerable to the whims of the acquirer.

Rule 10: Team play. In the end, success was about Rule 10, the importance of uniting the best of both teams to evolve a sustaining culture. That required HGTV's senior team spending a lot of time in New York and bringing many of Food's senior members to Knoxville, so we could see how we all might gel. Most of their senior team did depart, but many remained for years with us, and some key staffers remain today.

Everyday Team Plays

You often hear the words *team player* used to describe people in your organization. Perhaps you're one of those. It wouldn't surprise me, because women are excellent team players. We know how to play all kinds of supporting roles because our lives as a whole are a composite of roles. Back to the queen chess piece analogy, we're beings who can move all over the board, whether it's work, or life outside of it. As workers, you may perhaps be *too* good a team player, because the reinforcement that comes with being labeled as such stalls you from making key offensive moves, as discussed in Chapter 3. It's necessary for most people to be considered team players to advance, but what's also critical is a willingness to take risks and to exhibit leadership. The beauty of becoming a leader in your organization is that you now get to play many roles, including that foundation role of team player.

There are everyday matters that occur at work that require you, as a senior staffer, to rotate through the various roles you play. You move from teammate, to coach, and sometimes to referee. One good practice that did come from NBC began with its owners, General Electric, who did "workouts" when people or cultural values came into conflict with one another. We did these at SNI, which meant we would gather a team that was having dysfunction of some sort— usually the result of personality conflicts—into a room, and we would bring in an outside moderator to get the issues aired and resolved before anyone could leave the room. (Bathroom breaks were allowed.) Sometimes members of our senior team would sit in to help facilitate it, and sometimes a few senior folks alone would handle the more troubling culture clashes.

We tackled a team dysfunction that sprang from religious tensions. Other than some senior members, the bulk of our HGTV workforce was fairly homogenous, especially regarding religion. Most were from the South and were Christian. After a couple of years we began pulling in talent from other parts of the country, and after the Food purchase we found ourselves almost overnight with a large base of New York employees. The senior team spent an inordinate amount of time beginning about the first of November with meetings devoted to what the holiday cards should say, whether putting a Christmas tree in the lobby is making a religious statement, and my personal favorite, discussions of Christian imagery in our programming.

A group of Knoxville-based employees expressed concerns that our programming folks were purposely leaving out Christian symbols in the holiday programming we aired. They felt we were making an anti-Christian message. Our head programming executive, Ed Spray, along with Ken and me, got in a room with three representatives from this group, and we addressed it head-on. We sat and listened for a while. Then Ed explained why that wasn't so and showed them how we balanced our religious programming decisions. I said very little and just listened. The three staffers were fine with the outcome of the meeting, and it occurred to me how important just getting in a room and *listening* was to good team play.

A little while later our executive vice president of programming, Burton Jablin (who now runs SNI), went to visit Carol Duvall, one of our stars, who was known as the Queen of Crafts to all her viewing fans. Carol had a big, passionate following, and her viewers would often send her crafts for possible use on her show. When Burton went to see Carol, she was discussing her upcoming holiday shows, and she displayed two nativity scenes she wanted to put on the air. These projects departed quite notably from traditional nativity scenes. One was made with . . . well, penguins, and the other with billiard balls. She showed them to Burton, who said, "You know, Carol, I'm Jewish and can't claim to know a lot about these things. But I'm guessing some Christians might be offended by seeing Jesus depicted as a baby penguin or a pool ball."

Team harmony restored; crisis averted.

Sometimes being a team player means putting the needs of the team first. In some cases, this may mean playing a team role you think you've outgrown. Deanna Mulligan, CEO of Guardian Life Insurance, lists "Master and Move Up" as one of the myths about how women can advance in the workplace. It's a myth, she says, that women must move up as quickly as possible. Instead, she says, women should balance and consider the needs of their own careers with the needs of the teams they are on. When you learn a job, she says, stay long enough to leave it better than you found it. Put into it what you got out of it. That's part of team play—the give and take of help. It's a reminder that team play may not always have you as a team leader.

And that's not only fine, that's a good way to help your own prospects down the road.

Picking the Right Team

When it comes to picking the right team—or company—to join, women have a lot at stake. While most men may be able to make a purely career-oriented choice, many women will have to consider the other noncareer responsibilities in their lives. If it applies to you, look for companies that express family-friendly values on their websites and in their actions. Then, in the interview process, dig deeper to get examples of how the company translates these values into real life. In an artfully assertive way, ask HR to give you examples. If you and the company are interested in each other, ask to meet a few others in the organization, especially women, and ask them how the company lives its values.

Finally, look for companies that land on best lists to work for women, which are published and updated annually.

It's not a guarantee. Once inside a company, you may still find that your division head is not adhering to what you thought you were buying into when agreeing to come on board. This is another reason to consider some cross-training in other areas that could use your skill sets and where there is more team chemistry.

The best team chemistry is about your team gelling, and it's also about fitting in well with the culture of a place. I recall one night when I was working at CNBC, and we were in the midst of some tough contract negotiations. Many of us were pulling all-nighters as we pressed toward a deadline for these to be completed. I had my work in good shape and headed home around 7:00 that night. My boss called me at 9:00 and wanted to know why I wasn't in the office, even though he knew my deals had been completed. My corporate supervisors also knew I had a newborn son and had missed many days and nights with him to do the contract work. It struck me as strange and inconsistent, given that I had been allowed time overseas to adopt Andrew, when GE didn't have such a policy in place. In any event, this was one of the last episodes that convinced me the NBC culture wasn't a good fit.

Contrast that with the culture at HGTV. As we were building the business, we had many visitors who came to Knoxville for potential partnership talks of various kinds. Advertisers, cable operators, and broadcasters, who had heard of our early success, wanted to know more about us. I was traveling about 70 percent of the time in those days, and while I'm thankful my husband, Bill, had agreed to be a stay-at-home dad, I still missed my morning and evening time with my son. Ken knew this. He had no kids but, somehow, implicitly knew the tug and pull of being a working mom. Whenever we had visitors, we would then take them to dinner, and every time Ken would come into my office and say the same thing: "We're taking Company X to dinner and I'm inviting you, and I hope you say no." He always gave me an out. When I asked him about it recently, this is what he said:

My take on that was always: so we're at a dinner and somebody says, "Your chief operating officer's not here." And I could say, "Yeah, she's home with her family." It makes a statement about our company. We're not taking roll call here. If you abuse the system, the system will know and the company will know. You and I were trying to set a tone for this company; I wasn't being magnanimous.

The morning after a dinner I would seek out an update from whichever colleague had attended and was available to give me a debrief. I once read an interview with Sabrina Parsons, CEO of Palo Alto Software, and she said that not all management had to come to company meetings, but they're all invited. For those who couldn't attend the meeting, someone would send out a confidential recap.

These kinds of corporate behaviors give employees permission to find some work–life balance, and they reflect leadership's interest in treating its team like adults, not children who need constant supervision.

In the end, the right team chemistry is about the right company culture *for you*. As you consider where you want to plant your feet and grow your future, ask some questions of HR about the culture of the place. Do they have some core values? What do they mean? How are they operationalized? You don't have to come right out and declare, "I'm planning on having a family soon. How will you accommodate that?" Or "I have an infant at home. What provisions do you make for working mothers?" You don't need to sabotage the interview. Use artful assertiveness. By asking about the *culture* of the place, you'll begin to get your answers.

And if the company interests you and they want you, ask to meet one or two employees you haven't yet met, and ask them about the company's culture. You'll uncover a lot of what you need to know. Then, as we all do when we join a new company, you'll take a chance and trust that your instincts about the place are right.

HOME TEAM

Creating and managing a team is not just a workplace experience. Women especially may find themselves needing to craft and manage a home team. Many of the same issues come up—issues of changing roles and the need to often put the team success ahead of your own. That said, workplace teammates can be held accountable. Home teammates, not so much.

My husband, Bill, was a college instructor, and when we decided to start a family he agreed to become a stay-at-home dad. My career was taking off, and we both wanted one parent at home for child rearing. Bill was vigilant and loving, and a great diaper changer. But for some reason he volleyed the chore of potty training to me.

The timing of doing this worked well, as it was the December holidays, and I was in discussions with Scripps about becoming the number two employee for nascent HGTV. I took a whole three weeks off from NBC to ponder my career and to potty train our son.

I embraced potty training the way I did most things—with maniacal preparation. My aunt Carrie had lent me her dog-eared, coffee-stained potty-training book. It said to strategically locate a plastic potty where your child likes to play and to purchase various colored drinks with lots of sugar (recall this was the 1990s). This way you could do double-duty, teaching your child his colors while having him guzzle beverages nonstop to force the bladder relief part.

I purchased not one, but four plastic potties and placed them in strategic sites throughout the house. All of this was planned out like military maneuvers, as if a three-year-old could follow orders and relieve himself on command. He certainly was not willing to be held accountable for his bathroom business!

While Andrew was having accidents all over the place, choosing everywhere but my targeted sites for his business, the doorbell rang. It was FedEx with an employment contract from Scripps making me executive vice president of HGTV and allowing me the potential to make more than I'd ever made in my life, if I performed. In that moment I remember laughing at the irony of how normal family life butts up (purposeful choice of words) against the thrilling, engrossing ride of one's career, and the choices we make every day between the two.

Girlfriends, a Best-Kept Secret

The home team does not just mean your family. One of the secrets to work–life balance is having girlfriends. I had a few, but other women I know prioritized their female friendships much better than I did. My friend Bridget Baker, former president of NBC Cable Distribution, had a Thursday night book club with female friends, and if she was in town, she never missed it. She had three children but felt time with women friends gave her balance. They helped her see herself and her life choices more objectively. They gave her honesty, understanding, and care. These friends were her network. Men see networking as a part of their job; why don't we? Girlfriends are a critical part of your home team, along with family and community. They get you because they are you.

If I had had a better girlfriend network during my peak work years, they would have helped me see how much I enjoyed working and how it actually made me a better mom. I would have heard something outside my own guilt-ridden head. Girlfriends hold up a mirror and help you to see yourself much better. They offer validation, compassion, and honesty. The best female friends will tell you off if you're out of line, then hug you.

My friend Joanne Cuddihee has worked her whole life at Anheuser-Busch in various management roles. It took some real staying power to remain in such a male-dominated company. Recently she sent me an article that came from Stanford University about the importance of girlfriends to your health. Stanford had a speaker who gave a lecture about how women connect to form support systems that help one another deal with stress and tough life experiences. This quality girlfriend time helps women create more serotonin, a neurotransmitter that helps naturally combat sadness and depression.

Your home team is your family, girlfriends, other close friends, and community. This group of people makes you whole, keeps you honest, and allows you to have the emotional balance to suit up for work every day. They allow you to win at home and to win in the workplace.

Work–Life Balance in Phases, in the Moment, and on Parallel Tracks

Sheryl Sandberg, COO of Facebook and author of *Lean In*, gave voice to one important reason women do not advance in executive ranks: Worried about their ability to manage work–family balance, they take themselves out of the running. They lean out, she says. And they do so, in part, because they believe they can't have it all.

This "all" that everyone seems to want, but no one can have, has been a big issue for women in the workforce. And while many issues rise up to challenge us and many are out of our control, Sheryl is not wrong. Work–family balance is, for many women, a mental game.

My ninety-six-year-old, somewhat dramatic aunt Rachel would always say to me: "You're your own worst enemy! You want to be everything all at the same time!" Her words hit home. In talking with some female friends in senior roles, they revealed to me something called the 24-Hour Rule, which goes like this: With only 24 hours in a day, there is no such thing as having perfect balance in both work and life. And because the system's imperfect, doing your best is *enough*.

You can have balance in *phases* of life and balance in the *moment*. Regarding the former, you can look at your life as a composite of phases—your intense career-driven phase with that as a priority, and then child rearing as another phase with that as the priority. Something has to give with these two enormous jobs, and to have any sanity you must find peace with making these choices. Early childhood years and teen years are equally challenging and can call for hands-on parenting, if this is what you choose to do. Seeing balance in phases allows you to push career and advancement goals in the sweet spots of mid-thirties through the early fifties (depending on when you have your children). That's what I did. I began pulling back at fifty-two years of age. I had enough self-actualization from work by then and wanted to greatly lessen my travel as Andrew hit his teen years.

Balance in the *moment* is being able to give your focus and best efforts to what you are doing at that very moment. No distractions. When you're at work, you practice training yourself to be truly present at meetings and with managing your projects. When you leave work, your priority is home and its incumbent duties. You may take work home, but it means home duties, like time with kids, get done first.

These two reasonable approaches to work and life aren't foolproof or perfect, but they can more readily reconcile the competing forces of home and work. I recall reading a woman's account of the challenges around home and work balance. She was so snowed under at home she'd set the microwave timer with the same numbers, like 22, because that was quicker than hitting separate buttons for the number 20. What a way to live.

The third approach is just to take a *parallel track* with both home and work, and remarkably, I'm finding that more women are finding peace with this. First of all, kids are more resilient than parents give them credit for. The women who did the *parallel track* confirmed that to me time and again, and I saw how well their kids turned out. When stressed, the moms would say, "I'm doing the best I can do" and that little mental pep talk worked for them. Sometimes it could be messy, but they would reconcile that while there are juggling and tradeoffs, they're doing their best at both, and that's enough. They refer to sometimes feeling off-balance and seem to know it, which is when they step up work focus or step up home focus. They do a good job living the 24-Hour Rule.

All of these methods work best when women are not the only ones trying. It is a team effort. It requires a work team and a home team, and a woman's willingness to play changing roles in both. Sheryl Sandberg describes her efforts to negotiate with her work team for the right to leave the office at 5:30 and then log in additional work hours after her young children were in bed. Angela Braly, former CEO of WellPoint, had a husband willing to lead the home team, staying home to spearhead the raising of the kids. PepsiCo's CEO Indra Nooyi relied on help from her mom—even when it meant her mom was more concerned about reminding Indra to bring home milk than she was about Indra's recent promotion.

What do these women show you? They illustrate that life is really a state of shifting priorities. You can't have it all every moment of the day any more than you can be it all every moment of the day. A full life requires that you shift focus when necessary. And build great teams around you.

I wouldn't describe myself as having absolute peace given this tug and pull, but I did my best. I got great comfort with the routines that I established with Andrew. When I was not traveling, I always had breakfast with him, and I always put him to bed at night. On the weekends we did a lot of one-on-one, and of course a lot of family time with Bill. This kind of time management with kids is what good working dads do too. They make time with their kids when not at work their top priority. This models for children what a working mom or dad looks like, with its accountabilities as well as its joys.

How to Analyze Rain Delays

In baseball there are often rain delays that occur after the game's already begun. The umps see lightning or torrential rain, so they call for a rain delay. If you're the starting pitcher, your coach will likely not let you back into the game when it starts up again because your arm has gone cold, and it risks injuries. It doesn't mean you won't start in a future game, but you're out for this one. This is a good metaphor for pulling out of the workplace to rear kids. You've been in the workplace for a while; the game has begun. Nature—be it rain or having children—pulls you off the field for a time. The difference is that with kids, some of us have a choice to keep playing or to pull out. For others, we must work for economic reasons. For them, there is no choice. If you *do* have a choice and you're pulled in both directions, work and home, how do you make it?

We can tend to glamorize things we're considering, as they look pretty good from a distance. My stay-at-home friends who never worked would sometimes express envy about the travel I did. I hated the travel; they wished for it. Those of us working can see full-time motherhood as something we yearn for: less stress, no deadlines, and really comfortable clothes. Of course there's a little truth and a little myth in both of these scenarios.

When making the choice to pull out, the first thing I would advise is to seek the counsel of friends you trust. Speak with women who have stayed working, and those who have pulled out. Gather their experiences so you can learn from them. Next, get feedback on yourself from others you trust. It could be girlfriends, siblings, a church leader. It needs to be someone who can tell you, with artful assertiveness, what he or she believes about you and what drives you. You're looking for an honest appraisal here. I was lucky that Bill offered to be the primary parent, as I didn't think to go to friends who could objectively tell me the truth: that I'd be a better worker than a stay-at-home mom. I had proved to myself I could do the work role well, and it was very gratifying and rewarding. I just couldn't picture myself being at home with kids and doing that well. It's a hard job! This was the only truth I knew at the time, and it propelled me to keep working.

Then you'll need some quiet time to reflect on questions such as these: What am I good at? What do I love to do? How much can I take on, and can I depend on others (spouse, hired support) to help me if I stay working? How far do I honestly want to go up the ladder? Will my self-image suffer without a salary and identity outside the home? Will my spouse still see me as an intellectual equal, or will he see me through the lens of gender role traditionalism if I stay at home? Can I look at this decision through the lens of life phases? Can I find peace regardless of the decision? Some of the answers come from your instincts and intuition. They're feelings that involve the heart and soul, not data that can be analyzed. It's important to take time for your own reflection.

Going through a process like this will, I hope, be illuminating. Ultimately, though, you can't know the hard truth until you experience it. Life is a series of choices we make each day. We do our homework and take some time for some quiet reflection. Then it's time to make a choice, and to live with it.

Stay-at-Home Dads

Coco Chanel once said, "There is time for work. And there is time for love. That leaves no other time." Well, Coco, someone still has to find the time to take out the garbage and load the dishwasher. As mentioned earlier, in my family that became my husband, Bill. He was a college instructor; I was a person rising in business making quite a bit more in salary. After lots of discussion, Bill offered to be our baby's primary caregiver.

When Andrew was five years old, a letter came from his kindergarten that said, "Andrew Packard has 14 tardies and this will go on his permanent record." Turns out Bill didn't know there were different rules for kindergarten than there were for preschool. He was just hanging around in the morning with Andrew, two guys in their underwear watching cartoons until they felt like heading to kindergarten.

Much of the stay-at-home parenting didn't come naturally to Bill, but I don't know that it comes naturally to all women either. I've read about female sexism when the question of stay-at-home dads is vetted. This is when women consider themselves equal to men at work but better at home. Many tasks involved in child-rearing may come more naturally to women than to men, but even if that's true, women practicing female sexism will never find peace in the work–life balance conundrum. They will try to be in both places at the same time, doing a perfect job at both. And making everyone around them miserable. It's just not possible.

Given Bill's field had been business and he had owned a small business himself, he played an important coaching role for me in my work, especially with my contract negotiations. I came to understand brinksmanship much better through Bill's eyes. He helped me understand the concept of negotiating mano a mano because, after all, I wasn't a mano. It helped him use his brain, and it helped me vet work issues with a fresh set of eyes.

As I work with women today I'm finding more have husbands who are staying home with the kids. The decision to do this can be a very tough one for a man, as there is still a social stigma attached to men being home with kids versus doing outside work. It takes a man who's comfortable in his own skin to handle it well. And it takes you, having the empathy to understand and to not put your relationship behind work and kids. Try to be vigilant about that. It won't be perfect—life never is. But if you're vigilant and things get out of balance, what matters is having open channels between you and your spouse or partner, so resentments don't build.

YOUR TURN

Work Team

1. The best work cultures are built on trust, because they're the ones that have the foundation to sustain themselves over time. Ask yourself if you work in one of these and, if not, be sure the place is a good fit for you.

2. There are ample opportunities to apply the gamer rules if you're a part of a merger. Don't be reactionary; manage your emotions and rely on the ten rules as your best filter and guide to the right behavior.

3. If work–life balance is something you seek, know there are

companies whose leadership values that (see page 221). If you've been at your place of work for a while you likely know if yours is one of them. If you're just seeking a new job, you can learn about a company's work–life values by asking HR and company employees about the culture of the place.

Home Team

4. Learn and apply the 24-Hour Rule—with only 24 hours in a day, there is no perfect work–life solution. In an imperfect world, all you can do is your best. And that is enough.

5. Indulging the thought that "If only I were with my kids" when you're working is a surefire way to experience guilt and pain. Why put yourself through it?

6. Establishing routines with your children is rewarding for both you and them. Kids need routines and consistency as much as you.

7. Girlfriends are the best-kept secret of finding some work–life balance!

8. If you are considering pulling out of your career to parent full-time, it's important to do some front-end work and then take the time to think about it. This decision should not be made impulsively. Use your personal network to help guide you.

9. If your spouse becomes a stay-at-home dad, use his brain and instincts to work through challenging work situations. Have him help you by discussing issues and offering guidance from time to time. This helps both of you. Also try to be vigilant to not put time with your partner after kids and work, so resentments don't build.

Epilogue

Game Changers

In a magazine article written in the early 1940s, male supervisors were given this advice when managing female employees:

1. Pick young married women. They have more of a sense of responsibility than their unmarried sisters. They're less likely to be flirtatious, they need the work or they wouldn't be doing it, and they still have the pep and interest to work hard and to deal with the public efficiently.

2. When you have to use older women, try to get ones who have worked outside the home at some time in their lives. Older women who have never contacted the public have a hard time adapting themselves and are inclined to be cantankerous and fussy.

3. General experience indicates that "husky" girls—those who are a little on the heavy side—are more even tempered and efficient than their underweight sisters.

And on it goes for a total of ten points, but I'll stop there. When I get really discouraged about women's progress toward the corner office, I pull out these tips to remind myself of how things have changed since this was written.

In 2014, Mary Barra was named the new CEO of General Motors. This is progress. I worked as an intern at GM, and that place was Stone Age male. The news of Mary's ascension helps me have a more positive heart toward our progress, but we still have such a long way to go.

WOMEN'S ACCOUNTABILITY TO WOMEN

Institutionally business is still pushing against the gale force winds of change. There is still inertia and discomfort with men promoting women. We're a different species. It takes more effort by men to collaborate and partner in the executive suite with women, so some rely on this type of rationale: She's not quite ready, or she doesn't have the depth of experience. But with the speed by which business needs to move today, nothing will ever get done with that mind-set. Women will never be ready. Projects in the pipeline will never launch. We need to have enough bravado to push ahead women and initiatives even if they're not fully baked to win in the workplace today.

While we're working to get male business leaders and business institutions to open up the pipeline to women, it's up to *us*, those of us women in authority today, to pull other women up the ladder. This means team play, Rule 10, with a focus on women and advancing them. We must be advocates to help women move up, if we're ever to see more gender balance in the senior ranks. In an interview with Irene Dorner, CEO of HSBC USA, a financial services company, she admitted to not working hard enough for women. She just kept her head down and pushed ahead in her career. I've heard this regret from other female CEOs too.

As senior women, we can't afford to keep our heads down. We're accountable to other women coming along and to the whole next generation of workers. We're accountable to our shareholders to provide the best operating results. Diversity around the executive table broadens debate that makes companies perform better. Endless data support that financial excellence is maximized with a diverse slate of senior officers.

FROM ATHLETE TO HEAD COACH

At SNI, I stepped up to become chief operating officer of an entire organization. I was, for the first time, the most senior woman in the organization and felt both accountable to other women and enthused about what I could do to make the organization a great one. I had garnered the requisite technical skills, and I had enough life experience to manage employees with emotional maturity and resilience. The big aha moment was realizing it was no longer about racking up my own personal wins. It was about the team and helping the entire organization be successful. I was certainly not alone in managing the team; Ken was CEO with ultimate authority, and the other founding members sat around the same table. We were a flat organization at the top and extremely collaborative in everything we did. But I felt a special accountability to the women as the company's most senior woman.

Here were some of the things I did, that you can do too if you're in a place of leadership:

Create core values that are genderless. One might argue the values we created at SNI skewed female, with such things as work–life balance, compassion/support, and shared responsibility among them. There was plenty of testosterone around the table that day when we created them, and I was the lone female. The lesson is if you are in a senior role on the ground floor of an organization, you can help to drive values that support less hierarchy, more focus on collaboration, and an appreciation for the tug and pull of work–life issues. Millennials and our newer workforces value these things, both men and women.

Put support programs in place. But what if you're not a startup company? There are still plenty of ways to build a more collaborative, work–life friendly environment. I began brown bag lunches called "Work/Life Balance Brown Bags." We found speakers who addressed balance issues and career challenges for women making their way. This is a simple way to signal to your team that you understand their life challenges and want to support them. In addition, our terrific HR head, Julie Cookson, and I put into place policies like flextime and job shares. We did this by calling established media companies and speaking to their HR folks about what they were doing in these areas. We then built consensus with the founding team to get these enacted. Review your flex benefits. These can be changed.

Sponsor women. In addition, I mentored and sponsored scores of women in the organization, offering support and exposure to other senior staff, and you should do this too. There's a difference between mentoring and sponsoring, and both are needed. To me, mentoring is having an open door to women, and men, who'd like your counsel and feedback. If you're an accessible leader, you'll be busy mentoring many. Sponsoring is proactive advocacy for certain women who can be leaders. This means—dare I say it?—if a man and a woman are both up for a bigger job, and they have equal talent, you choose the woman. Why wouldn't you choose her? This is what men do all the time for those they're sponsoring, and even those they're not. As women, our push for gender balance must be aggressive to be effective.

Let others lead. At age fifty-two, I moved out of the corner office. In sports parlance, I hung up my cleats. I didn't completely pull out, but I got agreement to change my scope of duties and to lessen my role, with the goal of pulling out in the next few years. There were many reasons for this. My dad, then suddenly my mom and sister had passed away, which shook me to the core. In the quiet of a grieving period, I envisioned a new chapter of life that, while unshaped, involved using my time in new ways. Moreover, our son was entering his teen years and I felt the need to get off the road. Yep, just when he wanted me around the least, I'd be there for him.

At that time many women were in senior roles at SNI, including women running three of our six brands, and occupying senior posts in many sales departments. The place was in good shape as far as gender diversity, which was not just my work. Ken and SNI's other executive team members were tremendous supporters of having a diverse executive table, for which I will always be grateful. It was time to let other women lead, and many, like Judy Girard, who wrote the book's foreword, were tireless advocates for women too. You don't need to be head coach forever. When you start to feel the pull of other things awaiting you, give others a chance to lead.

One woman, senior vice president of ad sales Karen Grinthal—a real keeper from the Food Network acquisition—sent me a nice note after a blog post I wrote. She said, "Thanks for leaving the ladder down, and climbing off the perch to make way for others." That note touched me, as others have from women over the years. I'm thankful that I could be in a position to make a difference.

OTHERS WHO ADVOCATED FOR WOMEN

Linda A. Bell, an economics professor at Barnard, did some research on women and workplace equity and wrote a paper on gender gap issues. Her findings confirmed that senior women supporting other women in their organizations leads to better pay for those women, and to more females populating senior roles. Advocacy by women, for women, is a key way to move the needle and diversify senior teams.

Susan Cameron announced she was leaving the CEO job at Reynolds American, a Fortune 500 company, in the summer of 2010. She was to depart her office early in 2011, when I first met her. (In 2014, she was brought back to resume the CEO role.) In 2011, she was one of only fifteen women who presided over a Fortune 500 company. I had begun to consult at Reynolds and wanted to meet Susan before she left. She was not only willing but came in one morning just to meet me and share her perspectives. Later she agreed to come and speak on a panel I was moderating—on her own dime. Susan reinforced what it means to be a senior woman willing to sponsor, support, and bring other women along.

I met Kathryn Swintek in South Africa in 2010 during an outreach function. She was to become C200's chair. She had a fascinating and successful ride in banking with Bank of New York Mellon and BNP Paribas. In 2008, when banking was imploding, she departed. She would do only prudent deals, and the leverage play during that time was too great for her to consider.

"There was nothing to win at the end of the day," she said.

On this particular trip to South Africa, my luggage was lost in

Amsterdam. Although I'd never met Kathryn before, she clothed me with her things until my bags arrived three days later. She literally gave me the shirt off her back.

Today she is managing partner in Golden Seeds, an investment fund that underwrites early-stage companies founded and managed by women.

"Venture capital is very male-dominated," she told me. "Women seeking capital aren't part of that club, so most women-owned businesses stay small. They don't seek investment capital because they don't have entrée." Golden Seeds is out to change that, and today they have over sixty companies and over $60 million invested.

WOMEN HELPING WOMEN: COMPANY AND INDUSTRY EFFORTS

Women are also helping women in companywide and industrywide initiatives. Here are three great examples.

You met Colleen Repplier, who found a way to be a good sport in Chapter 8 and from that got a big win. As president of Tyco Fire Protection Products, she transformed informal and localized women's networking activities into a global, companywide initiative called the Tyco's Women's Growth Network (WGN). She explains:

> Some of the field managers didn't support the local efforts and would say to female staffers, "You don't have time for that; you need to do your work." So that's where the network was when I came. And it seemed clear that what we really needed to do was to elevate the impact and the benefit of this initiative and to make sure it had

top-down support and sponsorship from our CEO and the senior leadership of Tyco.

Colleen pushed and got approval for corporate dollars, and then she put a structure in place. She brought together senior women from their operating units all over the world to HQ in Princeton, New Jersey, for a two-day summit. The agenda was full and tight. This included Tyco's CEO, Colleen's boss, and thirty-five top executives who attended parts of the meeting. I was there and keynoted the event, and I experienced firsthand all the energy in the room. Here's what happened later:

We asked for action steps from the participants and they said there should be a special review of talent that is for women, and we expanded that as a company to say women and people of color. There would be a dedicated talent review of high potential diverse candidates, which would better expose these people to our executive team. Then we would look at open jobs and try to look for matches between the candidates and the open jobs because the matching process just didn't happen naturally.

Due to that process, one of Colleen's direct reports, a promising young talent, got a big new job running an operation with a multimillion-dollar P&L. Colleen's actions and advocacy for women have led directly to bigger jobs for the Tyco women.

Chip maker Texas Instruments identifies and coaches promising female engineers for advancement to key operating areas of the company through a program called Women's P&L Initiative. They help develop women's leadership skills required for line management jobs. I love this example because the intent is perfectly clear: These women are to be moved into line positions, where one can influence change, and where one prepares for running a company.

You met Ann Drake, CEO of DSC Logistics, in Chapters 7 and 8. In 2013, she began an industrywide initiative for women in supply chain management called AWESOME (Achieving Women's Excellence in Supply Chain Operations, Management, and Education). Launched in January 2013, she identified more than 400 women who were senior women in the supply chain field and created a daylong symposium to which over 200 attendees came. She laid out three goals: (1) develop a network, (2) address the issues and challenges that affect women's ability to advance their leadership roles, and (3) effectively and dramatically change the landscape of women's leadership in supply chain management.

Ann held two events in 2013, and she and her cross-industry AWESOME council are putting together future activities from what they have learned. When I asked Ann what the participants are getting out of it, she said:

Women get confidence, they get connections, somebody to talk to, kindred spirits. Even today I had a meeting inside my company with seven of our mid- to upper-level women leaders who are participating and helping me with AWESOME. When I walked into the meeting, the energy was there. I had just come from an

important industry meeting where out of eighteen people in the
room, there was only one other woman besides me. We need AWE-
SOME.

Ann acknowledges that changing the practices of an entire industry is a herculean task, but she's up for the challenge. And in the
meantime she and her AWESOME team give hope and support to
other women in supply chain management.

STORMING THE BOARDS

C200 friend Jan Babiak is former global managing partner at Ernst
& Young and now is a member of many corporate boards, including
Walgreens. She began an initiative called Project Starfish. She has
collected more than 200 résumés from board-qualified women looking for board seats, and since she gets many calls for board work,
she can refer women. Getting on boards, especially of large, publicly
traded companies, can be very tough, partly because there is limited
board member rotation in the United States. She does all she can to
connect boards to the abundance of diverse talent available. Other
C200 friends such as Phoebe Wood, Pepsi board member, aggressively circulate women's bios when calls come into them. Phoebe
also identifies and organizes female business talent in her community
of Louisville and coaches them, financially invests in their ideas, and
provides contacts for them. Her coaching message is to think beyond
their local roots, to play beyond the competition they face there. She
pushes women to think big in every quarterly meeting they have
together, and she gives examples of what the larger playing field can
offer for their success.

THE GAME IS ON

There is great promise in what many female leaders are doing to support and grow women. Still, a lot of work lies ahead for those of us in a position to affect change, and to influence more gender balance in C-suite roles. This work will positively impact women who have been in the workplace many years and who have been pushing up against institutional inertia.

From a generational standpoint, there's great promise too. Many of my interviewees acknowledged that today, in our newest generation of female workers, they're seeing more confidence and a comfort with competitive expression. This generation is chock-full of the video gamer traits like optimism, social connectedness, and wanting their companies to stand for something, to have a greater meaning. They don't shy away from taking seminars to further themselves, like learning financial principles described in Chapter 1. They're open to understanding effective communication, such as asking with artful assertiveness, a trait discussed in Chapter 3. As for work dress, let's just say there's a lot of creative expression in this bunch. They'll find their way with a little soft guidance. With our newest workers too, there's not the inherent gender bias to catalog men and women in preset roles, which bodes well for the future. As far as emotional maturity goes, Rules 8 to 10, it's not surprising they have a lot of runway ahead. They need to learn how to develop trust alongside collegiality, and to discern the nuanced human interactions that come from having a few birthdays.

How much of this promise is due to Title IX, and more girls and young women playing team sports? Amy Miles, Regal Entertainment's young CEO, said she never knew a world before Title IX, and she's a strong, competitive leader. Women are learning to play sports as children and continue through their college years and even into the pro leagues now. This practice helps women get comfortable with the dynamics of winning and losing.

Says Joan Cronan, the first person you met in this book, "Most men who are successful back up and give credit to Little League Baseball or football or playing sports, but women don't today. I think in twenty years they will."

I hope some of these stories inspire you to not wait twenty years, when you can play to win today. In the meantime, like a night game's winning scoreboard, here's wishing you a life and career that lights up the sky.

Acknowledgments

First, let me thank the founding team of Scripps Networks Interactive. These men and I were on the same page in most things, and their support of women in senior roles made my work so much easier. Special thanks to my dear friend Ken Lowe, who had the HGTV idea, who mentored me, and who continues to be a dear friend. Other founders are Frank Gardner, Ed Spray, Burton Jablin, Mark Hale, Steve Newman, Jim Clayton, Channing Dawson, and Bob Baskerville.

Photo by Larry Nordwick for Scripps Networks Interactive

HGTV's founding team, Carmel, 2014

A little later we added Steve Gigliotti (it feels as if he were there from the beginning!) and Bob Gerrard. And to Judy Girard, who was a gentle shoulder of care as we were in our building days and who honored me by agreeing to write the foreword. Thanks too to Brooke Johnson, who called in some favors for me with the book.

Thanks to the larger founding team that sat around that small theater on launch morning as we welcomed HGTV into people's homes: John Ajamie, Randy Armstrong, Janet Baker, Natalie Banks, Bernard Bell, Laurie Benson, Melissa Birkholz, the late Phillip Boal, Rick Burleson, Suzanne Bussart, Stacey Case-Rumpsa, Fred Childress, Peggy Coker, Julie Cookson, John deGarmo, Mike Donavan, Sue Drew-Baskerville, Tammy Esser, Bryan Fails, Bob Fancher, Sharon Fleishacker, Peter Franks, Dan Frye, Terry Gaitlin, Carolyn Gay, Terry Giles, Jan Hatcher, Lisabeth Hayes, Carol Hicks, Debbie Holley, Doug Hurst, Kristen Jordan, Doug Klein, Rob Knolton, Jennifer Lay, Tracy Lay, Tim Lee, Annette Lindstrom-Brun, Cynthia Madson, Jill McNutt, Jamie Miller, Tim Motley, Greg Neal, Jill Olson, Sally Pangle, Sally Phillips, Mark Quinn, Willene Rea, Terri Reid, Elaine Roach, Jayne Roberts, Dusty Schmidt, Traci Schubert-Barrett, Vickie Shipp, Lorraine Taylor, Janet Thomson, Pam Treacy, Lori Troutt, Helen Turner, Jennifer Tyrrell, Robin Ulrich, Karen Underwood, Joanna Vaccarino-Case, April Valentine, Becky Vardell, Rodger Washington, Lisa Wells, Stephen Wiggens, the late Allen Williams, and Lauren Zavier.

And as the book was getting under way, special thanks to Mark Kroeger and Nancy Walters, who gave great feedback and assisted in so many ways.

As I was beginning to make my way in my career, I appreciate my HBO friends: the late Tony Cox and Stan Thomas, who taught me so very much about working with management; Bill Grumbles, who was a wonderful mentor; Mike Welch, who gave me my first job; Mike Jeffries, who was my first boss and trained me to understand technology. Later, the L.A. contingent was great. Janice Aull and I had all those late nights trying to figure out what our various bosses wanted us to be doing, then we'd do what we wanted anyway. To Patrick Moody, a friend who guided me (thank you, Patrick!) with this book.

To Joe Cohen, whose love, mentorship, and support got me through a tough time at Z Channel, and his wife, Rita. The Packard family loves you!

To my CNBC friends who were always just a phone call away and the best support: my Sedona pals Patricia Karpas and Laurie Lawrence; Caroline Vanderlip, Debbie Green, Larry Smith, and Bruce Ballard. To David Zazlav, who got me out of a few jams with clients and who offered his support for this book. And of course to my dear friend Bridget Baker.

Getting the book under way, thanks to Leslie Cauley, who urged me to write this; to Jennifer Josephy, who helped with the first proposal; and to Alice Schroeder, who connected me with David Black and his fabulous agency. My wonderful agent, Joy Tutela, who ditched me to have Florence but gave me a helpful Luke Thomas in her place during those months. David, your folks are top notch.

To my Penguin contact and editor, Jeanette Shaw, who saw something in my proposal that was worth pursuing and went for it. She's one great editor. And to John Duff, who gave counsel, and Marian Lizzi, who invented the word *cross-training*, which I hoisted for the book and gave her no credit. Marian, I am thanking you now! And to Lauren Becker, who was terrific in Jeanette's absence. Also to my editor, Ellen Neuborne, who gave me the rules of the road along with her edits.

To the men and women who were willing to talk candidly to me when I interviewed them, and provide such enriching stories: Frank Gardner, Ken Lowe, Joan Cronan, Amy Miles, Dean Gilbert, Alice Schroeder, Ronee Hagen, Ann Drake, Colleen Repplier, and Pat Mitchell.

Thanks to my two C200 PR girls who reached out to friends on my behalf, Beth Bronfman and Kathryn Swintek. And to Dennis Shuler, who connected me to some marvelous CEOs. Finally, to Gina Bianchini, who had me thinking larger than I otherwise would have. And to Amplify partners Allison McLean and Elizabeth Hazelton, what a team you are! Also to my friends Kristin and Jason Snow, who patiently teach me the tricks of social media.

To my E. W. Scripps friend Angie Epps, who gave her time and smart counsel to me.

There were many university people gracious with their time. From UT: Amy Cathy, and college students Katie I. Darnell and Kierra Warren, who did research for the book. At my alma mater MSU, to Meredith Jagutis and Lisa Parker, who organized my time at MSU with the book; to Dr. Janet Lillie, who's always been there for me; and for Dean Whitten, a great female leader and educator.

And finally to Dr. Pat Heim and Gail Evans, who pioneered concepts on women and gamesmanship.

References

Introduction

Gruenfeld, Deborah. "Power & Influence" [Discussion Guide]. Stanford, CA: Stanford Graduate School of Business. cdn-media.leanin.org/wp-content/uploads/2013/03/PowerInfluence3.15.pdf.

Rockoff, Jonathan D. "For Men, Election Is Like Big Game." *Wall Street Journal*, November 5, 2012. online.wsj.com/news/articles/SB100014240529702 03347104578101322736500776.

Society of Women Engineers, Columbia University. "Success and Likability Between Genders." *Aspire Advance Achieve* [Tumblr]. columbiaswe.tumblr.com/post/48049234044/success-and-likability-between-genders.

Sotomayor, Sonya. *My Beloved World*. New York: Knopf, 2013.

Trudeau, Michelle. "Video Games Boost Brain Power, Multitasking Skills," *National Public Radio*, December 20, 2010.

Chapter 1: It Starts with Conditioning

Barsh, Joanna and Lareina Yee. "Unlocking the Full Potential of Women at Work." *Wall Street Journal* Special Report, April 30, 2012. mckinsey.com/careers/women/~/media/Reports/Women/2012%20WSJ%20Women%20in%20the%20Economy%20white%20paper%20FINAL.ashx.

Bartiromo, Maria. "Starbucks' Schultz Eyes Global Growth." *USA Today*, September 16, 2013. usatoday.com/story/money/columnist/bartiromo/2013/09/15/starbucks-bartiromo-schultz-coffee/2809663.

Chapter 2: Play It Cool

"Big Girls Don't Cry." *Stylist. stylist.*co.uk/stylist-network/big-girls-dont-cry.

Branson, Richard. "Nice Guys Can Finish First." *Entrepreneur,* 2010. entrepreneur.com/article/217309.

Brizendine, Louann. *The Female Brain.* New York: Broadway Books, 2006, p. 279.

Favate, Sam. "Yale Law Study Finds Gender Imbalance in Student Participation." *Law Blog,* April 24, 2012. blogs.wsj.com/law/2012/04/24/yale-law -study-finds-gender-imbalance-in-student-participation.

Gay, Jason. "Let's Be Cool Like Mariano Rivera." *Wall Street Journal,* July 17, 2013. online.wsj.com/news/articles/SB1000142412788732444481045786120 10583001922.

Gregoire, Carolyn. "The Daily Habit of These Outrageously Successful People." *Huffington Post,* July 5, 2013. huffingtonpost.com/2013/07/05/business -meditation-executives-meditate_n_3528731.html.

Lockhart, Jhaneel and Melanie Hicken. "14 Executives Who Swear by Meditation." *Business Insider,* May 9, 2012. businessinsider.com/ceos-who -meditate-2012-5?op=1#ixzz363lkMUdq.

Chapter 3: Learn to Play Offense

Orbanes, Philip E. *Monopoly, Money, and You: How to Profit from the Game's Secrets of Success.* New York: McGraw-Hill, 2013.

Zernike, Kate. "Nancy Pelosi Is Ready to Be Voice of the Majority." *New York Times,* November 9, 2006. nytimes.com/2006/11/09/us/politics/09pelosi .html?_r=0.

Chapter 4: Master the Strategies of Brinksmanship

Fiorina, Carly. *Tough Choices: A Memoir.* New York: Portfolio, 2006.

McCarthy, Michael. "Lance Armstrong Blew His Last Chance, Experts Say," *Advertising Age,* January 19, 2013.

Chapter 5: Build Your Fan Club

Bryant, Adam. "Four Executives on Succeeding in Business as a Woman." *New York Times*, October 12, 2013. nytimes.com/interactive/2013/10/13/business/women-corner-office.html?_r=0.

Dalenberg, Alex. "What Improv Comedy Taught Twitter's CEO about Business." *Upstart Business Journal*, May 6, 2013. upstart.bizjournals.com/multimedia/videos/2013/05/twitter-ceos-biz-lessons-from-the-improv.html.

Fiorina, Carly. *Tough Choices: A Memoir.* New York: Portfolio, 2006.

Gostick, Adrian and Scott Christopher. *The Levity Effect: Why It Pays to Lighten Up.* Hoboken, NJ: Wiley, 2008.

Howard, Caroline, with Kate Pierce, Mehrunnisa Wani, and Chris Smith. "100 Women Who Lead the World." *Forbes*, May 28, 2014. forbes.com/profile/susan-wojcicki.

Markowitz, Eric. "Brilliant Leaders Use This Type of Humor (Hint: Think Woody Allen)." *Inc.com*, June 2013. inc.com/magazine/201306/eric-markowitz/humor-self-deprecation-leaders.html.

Miller, Claire Cain. "Google Appoints Its Most Senior Woman to Run YouTube." Bits [Blog]. *New York Times*, February 5, 2014. bits.blogs.nytimes.com/2014/02/05/google-appoints-its-most-senior-woman-to-run-youtube.

Moore, Robert J. "5 Improv Comedy Skills That Made Me a Better CEO." The Data Point [Blog], October 16, 2013. blog.rjmetrics.com/2013/10/16/5-improv-comedy-skills-that-made-me-a-better-ceo.

Schroeder, Alice. *The Snowball: Warren Buffett and the Business of Life.* New York: Bantam, 2008.

"Stress and Your Heart." *Harvard Women's Health Watch*, December 2013. health.harvard.edu/newsletters/Harvard_Womens_Health_Watch/2013/December/stress-and-your-heart?utm_source=womens&utm_medium=pressrelease&utm_campaign=womens1213.

Swartz, Jon. "Yahoo CEO's Pregnancy Overshadows Flat Revenue." *USA Today*, July 18, 1012. usatoday30.usatoday.com/tech/news/story/2012-07-17/yahoo-earnings-marissa-mayer/56285424/1.

"Words from the Top." *Wall Street Journal*, May 17, 2012. online.wsj.com/news/articles/SB10001424052702303360504577410660795002898.

Chapter 6: Practice, Practice, Practice

Bateson, Mary Catherine. *Composing a Life.* New York: Grove Press, 2001.

Bennett, Jeff and Joann S. Lublin. "At GM, New Chairman Won't Sit Still." *Wall Street Journal*, February 5, 2014. online.wsj.com/news/articles/SB30001424052702304851104579361210926045486.

Brown, Paul B. "Shortsighted Management." *New York Times*, November 24, 2007. nytimes.com/2007/11/24/business/24offline.html.

Hymowitz, Carol. "They Ponder Layoffs, but Executives Still Face Gaps in Talent." *Wall Street Journal*, January 2008. online.wsj.com/ad/article/oracle_ponder_layoffs.html.

U.S. Bureau of Labor Statistics. "Number of Jobs Held, Labor Market Activity, and Earnings Growth Among the Youngest Baby Boomers: Results from a Longitudinal Survey." Press Release, July 25, 2012. www.bls.gov/news.release/nlsoy.nr0.htm.

Chapter 7: Suit Up

Fiorina, Carly. *Tough Choices: A Memoir.* New York: Portfolio, 2006.

Galbraith, Sasha. "Learning to Believe in Herself, in High Tops or Heels." *Huffington Post Business*, June 17, 2014. huffingtonpost.com/dr-sasha-galbraith/learning-to-believe-in-he_b_5500855.html.

Chapter 9: Show True Grit

Coutu, Diane L. "How Resilience Works." *Harvard Business Review*, May 2002. hbr.org/2002/05/how-resilience-works/ar/1.

Van Deusen, Amy. "The Greatest Moments in Olympic Gymnastics History." About.com. gymnastics.about.com/od/majorcompetitions/tp/greatestmoments.htm.

Chapter 10: Be a Team Player

"Words from the Top." *Wall Street Journal*, May 17, 2012. online.wsj.com/news/articles/SB10001424052702303360504577410660795002898.

Sandberg, Sheryl and Nell Scovell. *Lean In: Women, Work, and the Will to Lead.* New York: Knopf, 2013.

"Most Powerful Moms: America's CEOs." *Working Mother,* 2013. working mother.com/most-powerful-moms/most-powerful-moms-americas-ceos.

Bryant, Adam. "A Start-Up Spirit, Without the 18-Hour Days." *New York Times,* April 11, 2013. nytimes.com/2013/04/12/business/a-start-up-spirit -without-the-18-hour-days.html?_r=0.

Bradley, David. "Why PepsiCo CEO Indra Nooyi Can't Have It All?" *Economic Times,* July 3, 2014. articles.economictimes.indiatimes.com/2014-07-03/ news/51057580_1_directors-pepsico-ceo-indra-nooyi-milk.

Epilogue: Game Changers

Sanders, L. H. "Eleven Tips on Getting More Efficiency Out of Women Employees." *Transportation Magazine,* July 1943. snopes.com/language/ document/hiringwomen.asp.

Additional Resources

WHAT IS A LINE JOB?

What exactly is a line job? The details and responsibilities will vary by company and industry, but at its core, a line person is a rainmaker. It's the job in which you interact with the outside world and create value for your employer. It is typically a job with accountability for both revenue and expense of a team, area, or department. Some examples follow. I drew them from job descriptions posted by major companies in a variety of industries.

Sales Manager: Telecommunications

The Sales Manager leads a team of senior account executives to sell solutions that solve clients' business and IT needs. The Sales Manager directs and coaches the sales team in the sales process, manages customer satisfaction, mentors and develops direct reports, and builds relationships both internally and externally.

Director, Sourcing Strategy Lead: Pharmaceutical

Primary responsibility is to champion and secure value realization for all designated teams and spend categories, drive innovation in the supply chain, lead/support major strategic programs, and institutionalize these processes. The Director is responsible for supporting value creation and delivery, end-to-end across the value chain, and business strategy, while engaging as a strategic business partner. This position includes international work and requires extensive work with international colleagues. The Director leads procurement and supply management with the goal of driving revenue generation, cost reductions, and productivity improvements while at the same time maintaining or improving product quality and supplier service levels.

Director, Global Point of Sale Strategic Programs and Capabilities: Financial Services

Reporting to the Global VP of Distribution and Point of Sale strategy, the Director is accountable for a multimillion-dollar P&L and ongoing preferred relationship strategies. The objective of this team leader is to implement innovative point of sale products as well as manage supplier campaigns.

The primary responsibilities include communicating point of sale strategy to global audiences, developing digital products including new media and e-commerce ideas, leading projects with global impact, assessing new business opportunities, and managing vendors.

The Director will manage a team that delivers new products to support supplier and distribution strategies, works to develop campaigns that drive preferred supplier programs, and executes broader strategic priorities from the Director.

Software Sales Manager: Technology

The Software Sales Manager will meet and beat revenue targets on a quarterly basis; target key clients, identify decision makers, and leverage opportunities to promote and sell software products and services; and drive revenue by gaining an in-depth understanding of client needs and identifying opportunities within clients' organizations.

THE TEN BEST COMPANIES FOR WOMEN IN 2014 (*FORBES*)

1. IBM
2. Ernst & Young
3. Marriott
4. AstraZeneca
5. General Mills
6. Grant Thornton
7. KPMG
8. Procter & Gamble
9. State Farm
10. Verizon

WORKING MOTHER 2013 NAFE TOP COMPANIES FOR EXECUTIVE WOMEN

1. Abbott
2. AstraZeneca
3. General Mills
4. IBM
5. Johnson & Johnson
6. KPMG
7. Marriott
8. Procter & Gamble
9. Prudential
10. State Farm

RESOURCES FOR BUILDING A GLOBAL CAREER

Print Media

- *Advertising Age*
- *Economist* and *Economist Intelligence Unit* (for economic fore-casting)
- *Financial Times*
- *Forbes*
- *Fortune*
- George Friedman, author, futurist, and political scientist

- *New York Times* (general reading); Sunday Travel (exposes you to the beauty and knowledge of personal travel)
- *Wall Street Journal*

Websites

- City sites (for example, miamidade.gov)
- Frommers.com and michelintravel.com (travel sites)
- State.gov; trade.gov (U.S. Department of State)
- State sites (for example, myflorida.com)
- TED.com
- Wikipedia (especially for a country's history, leadership, and political profiles)

Places

- Foreign embassics (located in many large cities, for travel and business information)
- Universities (seek specialists in a country of interest in the history, art, and political science departments)

Group

- Council on Foreign Relations (consider joining)

RESOURCES FOR SPEAKING AND PRESENTATION

Books

Communication in General

Franklin Vocab System. *Franklin Executive Vocabulary for Effective Communication: 2180 Most Common Words for Business Communication*. Udaipur, India: CreateSpace Independent Publishing, 2013.

Gallo, Carmine. *10 Simple Secrets of the World's Greatest Business Communicators*. Naperville, IL: Sourcebooks Inc., 2006.

Klaus, Peggy. *The Hard Truth About Soft Skills: Workplace Lessons Smart People Wish They'd Learned Sooner*. New York: HarperCollins Publishers, 2007.

Murphy, Herta, Herbert Hildebrandt, and Jane Thomas. *Effective Business Communications*. London: McGraw-Hill Education (Europe), 1997.

Perkins, P. S. *The Art and Science of Communication: Tools for Effective Communication in the Workplace*. Hoboken, NJ: John Wiley & Sons, 2008.

Speaking

Carnegie, Dale. *How to Develop Self-Confidence and Influence People by Public Speaking*. New York: Pocket Books, 1998.

———. *Public Speaking for Success*. New York: Tarcher/Penguin, 2005.

———. *The Quick and Easy Way to Effective Speaking*. New York: Association Press, 1962.

Carroll, Kevin and Bob Elliott. *Make Your Point!: Speak Clearly and Concisely Anyplace, Anytime.* Bloomington, IN: AuthorHouse, 2005.

Chapman, Gary and Paul White. *The 5 Languages of Appreciation in the Workplace.* Chicago: Northfield, 2011.

Detz, Joan. *How to Write and Give a Speech.* New York: St. Martin's Press, 1992.

Detz, Joan. *It's Not What You Say, It's How You Say It.* New York: St. Martin's Griffin, 2000.

Fleming, Carol A. *It's the Way You Say It: Becoming Articulate, Well-Spoken, and Clear.* San Francisco: Berrett-Koehler Publishers, 2013.

Frank, Milo O. *How to Get Your Point Across in 30 Seconds or Less.* New York: Simon & Schuster, 1986.

Greenberg, David. *Simply Speaking!: The No-Sweat Way to Prepare and Deliver Presentations.* Atlanta, Georgia: Goldleaf Publications, 1997.

Toogood, Granville. *The New Articulate Executive: Look, Act, and Sound Like a Leader.* New York: McGraw-Hill, 2010.

Body Language

Goman, Carol Kinsey. *The Silent Language of Leaders: How Body Language Can Help—or Hurt—How You Lead.* San Francisco: Jossey-Bass, 2011.

Kay, Katty and Claire Shipman. *The Confidence Code: The Science and Art of Self-Assurance—What Women Should Know.* New York: HarperCollins, 2014.

Website

mindtools.com (essential skills for an excellent career)

SMEAC

SMEAC is the acronym for the standard five-paragraph order, which comes from the description of the order of operation of a mission:

1. Situation
2. Mission
3. Execution
4. Administration and logistics
5. Command and signal

This format is still used by the Marine Corps, but the army has been teaching SMEAC for several years. See also en.wikipedia.org/wiki/Five_paragraph_order.

NEGOTIATION

Margaret Neale, "Negotiation: Getting What You Want," youtube.com/watch?v=MXFpOWDAhvM